Felt & Fur

20 simple makes to sew

Felt & Fur

20 simple makes to sew

Emma Herian

CONTENTS

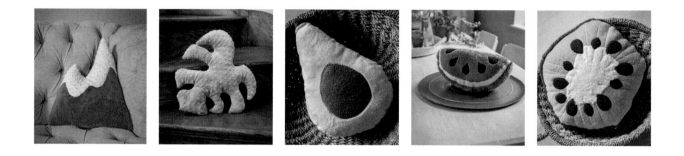

INTRODUCTION

Creativity has always been in my blood – learning how to knit on two pencils while listening to my teacher at story time is a prime example. Growing up watching and learning from my mother, who made us beautiful childhood dresses in Liberty fabrics and later pandered to one of my teenage phases by creating amazing Gothic outfits, it was inevitable that being able to sew would flow through my veins and end up being my career.

Over the years I have made countless dressing-up outfits for my children. Whether it was Roman and Tudor costumes for school history lessons, mermaid tails or superhero capes, I would always relish the challenge.

Over time I created a small business selling textile art, jewellery and toys, exhibiting at numerous fairs. This slowly evolved and eventually an opportunity arose to create and write craft tutorials for magazines and books.

'Plushie' is a term often used to describe a soft stuffed toy. It comes from the word 'plush', meaning a fabric, such as silk, cotton or wool, that has a long, soft nap (textured surface), making it extravagant, luxurious and abundantly rich. With the help of modern technology, these fabrics have developed over time and it is now possible to push the boundaries of the traditional soft toy with unusual prints and textures.

So with that in mind, I have used a combination of those soft, tactile fabrics – from dimpled and shaggy faux furs to felts and fleeces – and allowed my imagination to go a little wild in order to create a book filled with unique and modern interpretations of soft toys and cushions.

Felt & Fur will take you through the therapeutic process of sewing a variety of fun, cute and loveable items for you and your home, or to give as gifts. There are clear step-by-step instructions and photographs for each project, as well as tips for alternative methods and materials, and templates (found at the back of the book) to get you started off on the right foot.

At the beginning of the book you will find information and guidance on the tools and materials you'll need, along with a techniques section, which will explain in detail the methods used to complete the projects.

If you have a basic knowledge of sewing then there are plenty of projects to get you started; delve further into the book and you will find more elaborate ideas to stretch your skills.

Whatever your level of expertise, you'll find everything you need to help you create adorable plushies. Enjoy the process and have some fun!

Emma

TOOLS

From measuring and cutting tools to needles and pins, here are the essential tools needed for your felt and fur creations, along with some optional extras.

SEWING MACHINE

A basic sewing machine will be perfect for any of the projects in this book. Electric sewing machines are the best all-round machines, as they tend to have a variety of stitch patterns included, some of which will be useful in a few projects, but not essential. Your machine should also have the possibility to alter the tension and stitch length to allow for the different types of fabrics used. When it comes to sewing the plush fabric, set your machine for a longer stitch length and always test the stitching first on a scrap of fabric to make sure the length and tension achieves the best results.

Sewing machines usually have a universal presser foot that holds the fabric flat as it is fed through the machine and stitched. Due to the slippery nature of some of the fabrics used in the projects, a walking foot (sometimes referred to as an even feed foot) will be useful as it enables both layers of fabric to feed through the machine in unison.

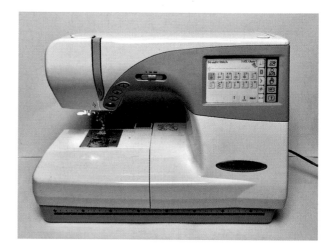

SEWING MACHINE

NEEDLES

SEWING MACHINE NEEDLES

There are a multitude of different types of sewing machine needles and they come in a range of sizes. The type you need depends on the fabric you are using. A universal 90/14 machine needle will be used for sewing the felt part of the projects in this book, but when it comes to sewing the soft plush and fleece fabrics it is recommended that you switch to a ballpoint tip 90/14 stretch needle, which are available to buy in most craft stores and online (see page 149).

HAND SEWING NEEDLES

There will be occasions when you'll be required to sew part of a project by hand or to add embroidered detail. Hand sewing needles are similar to machine needles, as the size and type depend on the fabric that is being sewn. Sharps are the most common general-purpose sewing needles, and have a short, round eye that provides added strength when sewing. A pack of universal assorted needles will usually have what you need for most of the projects in this book. I like to use a size 4 for the medium to heavy fabrics. For the decorative embroidered stitches used on the Cacti (see page 96) and Pizza Slice (see page 80), use an embroidery needle. Embroidery needles have a sharp tip to penetrate the thick felt fabric and a bigger eye, ideal for thicker thread.

PINS

Due to the nature of plush and fleece fabrics, and the likelihood of them slipping when sewing, pins are a very important item to have – and you will be using plenty.

WATER/AIR-SOLUBLE MARKER PEN

Use a water or air-soluble fabric marker pen directly onto fabric – it is a hassle-free way of marking important measurements directly onto the fabric without having to rub them out afterwards.

SCISSORS AND PINKING SHEARS

A pair of sharp scissors is a must for cutting the fabrics used in this book. It is a great idea to have a small pair, too, as they are perfect for snipping stray threads. When I created the decorative edges on the Llama's blankets (see page 56), the black Sushi seaweed wrap (see page 68) and the Lemon stem (see page 40), I used a pair of pinking shears. They create a zigzag pattern (instead of a straight edge) and work well when cutting felt.

PRINTER/PHOTOCOPIER AND PAPER

You will need a printer/photocopier to recreate the patterns for each project (see page 126). Before printing, do check at what percentage each one should be copied to recreate the exact size.

VACUUM CLEANER/LINT ROLLER

Plush and fur fabrics tend to shed a lot of fibres when cut. Give the fabric a good shake after cutting and then have a vacuum cleaner or lint roller handy to clear away the loose fibres before sewing. It is also recommended to vacuum the mechanism in and around the sewing machine in between projects to prevent clogging.

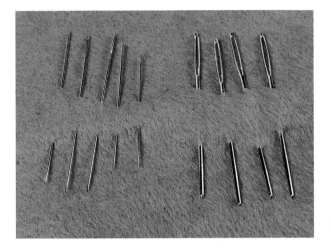

HAND SEWING NEEDLES

MISCELLANEOUS

Extra tools that are handy to have and use are: sticky tape to join patterns; pencil and string to draw a circle for the Iced Doughnut (see page 62); some tissue paper to prevent slipping and puckering of plush fabric when using a decorative stitch on the machine (see page 13); and a ruler and tape measure.

TIP

When cutting out a pattern and sewing with plush, faux fur and fleece fabrics, always keep the grain lines the same and be aware of their direction. This will help combat any problems you might encounter with the pile and stretch.

MATERIALS

You'll need a selection of fabrics, threads and other materials for the projects in this book. It's helpful to familiarize yourself with their properties and uses to know how to care for your project once it's complete.

CHOOSING YOUR MATERIALS

When making any plush toy or cushion for a child, safety is a key concern. Consider the age of the child you are making the item for and whether it will be suitable for them.

When buying your fabric, make sure you source it from a trustworthy fabric manufacturer who can guarantee the highest quality-control standards in the production of their fabrics. You should also ensure that the fabric is safe and hypoallergenic.

The type of fabric you choose is just as important. When it comes to plush fabric, the long-pile plush fabrics are not suitable for babies under 12 months of age, as any loose fibres can pose a choking hazard, so use a shorter-pile fabric instead. When choosing felt fabric, I recommend that you buy wool felt rather than acrylic felt, as it is naturally hypoallergenic and fire resistant. It is also very durable and less likely to bobble.

Toys for children should be sturdy and contain no small parts, so avoid attaching buttons for eyes/ noses if the plushie is being made for (or will be in close proximity to) babies or young children, as they are likely to pull them off and swallow them. To avoid such risks, embroider on or sew around felt eyes and other features with a short close appliqué stitch.

FABRICS

PLUSH

Most modern plush fabrics are manufactured from synthetic fibres, such as polyester, making them very soft, which is why plush fabric is also known as cuddle fabric. The height, thickness and direction of the soft pile adds a luxurious feel in a variety of textures. In this book you will be using a combination of plush fabrics that are smooth or textured, such as dimple, rose swirl and shaggy (very fluffy).

FAUX FUR

Similar to plush, faux fur is made from synthetic fibres, such as polyester and acrylic, and makes a fantastic alternative to real animal fur. Thanks to modern technology, the direction and height of the pile has evolved to create many types of textured faux fur, from a lambswool look and imitation scale effect to long-haired varieties, all of which are used in the various projects in this book.

FLEECE

Like plush fabric, fleece is a synthetic fabric usually made from polyester fibres. It is incredibly soft to the touch, stretchy and very durable. Fleece fabric can be smooth on one side and plush on the other, and either can be used as the 'right' side (see page 71). It is also available in a huge range of colours and can also come in a variety of thicknesses. Microfleece (a thin, soft, lightweight fabric) and polar fleece (a thick, dense, soft fabric) are two examples.

FELT

Felt is a versatile fabric that works well alongside the plush, fleece and faux fur fabrics. Felt can be made from either natural fibres, such as wool, or synthetic fibres, such as acrylic. Wool felt is likely to stretch more than synthetic felt, so bear that in mind. There are different thicknesses available, as well as some amazing colours. You can also find felt that has patterns printed on its surface, some of which you will be using in the Animal Masks project (see page 114), or is coated in glitter, such as the felt used for the Unicorn's mane (see page 120).

SOFT-TOY FILLING

The most common soft-toy filling you will find is polyester hollowfibre, which should always comply with fire safety regulations. This type of filling is ideal for the projects in this book, giving them a huggable and light feel once filled. If you are looking for allergy-free filler, you can use a hypoallergenic brand or use natural wool toy stuffing instead.

THREADS

SEWING THREADS

There are a variety of threads available for hand sewing or machine sewing, such as cotton, silk and polyester. Finding the right thread to use is quite important. I used the Gutermann brand of threads for the projects in this book, but you may prefer a different brand.

Polyester is an everyday thread that can be used in so many different types of projects, whether you are sewing by hand or using a machine. It has a small amount of give, which makes it ideal for stretch fabrics such as plush. It is a strong and durable thread and comes in a variety of colours, making it perfect for these cuddly projects.

EMBROIDERY THREADS

A couple of the projects require embroidery thread. I would recommend using a 100% cotton thread that has a slight gloss finish and comes as a six-strand thread, which can be separated. I used all six threads as one to create thick

stitching on the Cacti (see page 96), Kiwi Fruit (see page 34), Pizza Slice (see page 80) and Lemon (see page 40) projects.

OTHER MATERIALS

I have used other materials for various projects in this book, such as wide elastic for the Animal Masks (see page 114), pom-poms to decorate the Iced Doughnut (see page 62) and buttons for the Whale's eyes (see page 50). All these materials are available from any good arts or craft store or can be bought online (see p149).

FABRIC CARE

As many of the projects in this book are made from a combination of fabrics, including felt, it is advisable to gently handwash the item in cool water, using a small amount of mild detergent. Carefully squeeze out most of the water, then allow to air-dry.

For small spots and stains, first remove any residue (for something sticky like honey, try using the blunt edge of a knife), then gently wipe the area with a damp cloth that has been soaked in a mild detergent, making sure to wipe the fabric in one direction. Allow to air-dry.

For a general clean without the use of water, first go over the item with a vacuum cleaner to remove any dust, using a small nozzle with a thin sock placed over the end to prevent a strong suction. Then place the item in a plastic bag with at least half a cup of baking soda. Twist the top of the bag to seal and give it a good shake for at least two minutes. Leave the item in the bag for approximately 15 minutes – during which time any dirt will adhere to the baking soda and it will also deodorise the item – then remove the plushie and give it a shake.

BASIC TECHNIQUES

This section outlines the main techniques that you'll need to be familiar with to complete the projects in this book.

INVISIBLE STITCH

Before you start hand sewing an invisible stitch, make sure you're using a thread that matches the colour of the project, or as close as possible. If you can't find a thread that matches exactly, use a darker shade rather than a lighter one.

This invisible stitch is technically called a 'ladder stitch' and is best used to join two seams or to close an opening.

To close an opening, first secure the thread on one edge (if you knot the thread, hide this within the seam already sewn at the beginning) then sew a small stitch on the fold of the opposite edge. Return to the first edge and sew a similar stitch on that fold. Repeat the process along the whole opening and you will notice a ladder-like stitch will form between the two edges.

Gently pull the thread every now and then to tighten the stitch. Close the opening, hiding any evidence of the stitches, then fasten it off neatly within the fold of the seam and cut any stray threads.

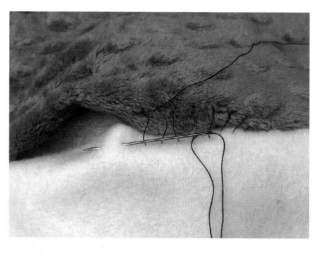

INVISIBLE STITCH

BACKSTITCH

A backstitch is usually used at the beginning and end of a seam to prevent the ends from unravelling and stretching out of shape. You will be using this stitch mainly when creating the opening into which you will place the toy filling.

BACKSTITCH

PINNING

To create a backstitch you simply sew a few stitches backwards and then a few forwards on top of the seam already sewn. This can be done either by using the reverse button on your sewing machine or lifting the sewing foot and pivoting the fabric around to face the other way.

PINNING

Plush and fleece fabrics are prone to shifting when cutting and sewing, so pins are your best friends if you don't want any mishaps. Use plenty of pins and place horizontally to the edge at least every ½in (1.5cm) to stabilize the fabric and prevent puckered seams, especially when sewing.

TISSUE PAPER TECHNIQUE

When sewing a tight stitch on the sewing machine, such as the decorative satin stitch, the stitches on a single layer of plush fabric can slip and pucker, resulting in a distorted line. To prevent this, pin a piece of tissue paper on the reverse of the fabric where you intend to sew, then sew the shape as intended.

When you have finished sewing, fasten off any stray threads and then gently tease the tissue paper away from the fabric; you should be left with a perfectly flat sewn line.

This technique can also be used between layers of fabric if you find that pins aren't enough to stop the fabric slipping.

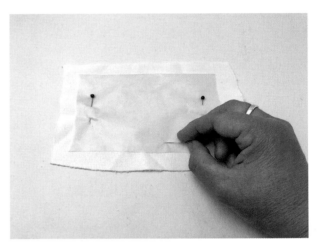

TISSUE PAPER TECHNIQUE (1)

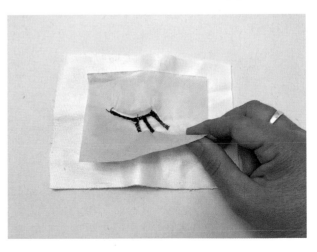

TISSUE PAPER TECHNIQUE (2)

DECORATIVE MACHINE STITCHES

It is always a good idea to practise the following stitches on a scrap of the fabric you intend to use before starting a project and decide whether the tissue paper technique will be required.

RUNNING STITCH

This stitch is your everyday sewing machine stitch, but when it comes to sewing with plush and fleece fabric you'll need to adjust the setting on your machine to a longer than normal stitch – something between 3mm and 3.5mm as this is best for stretchy fabric and prevents seams from puckering.

APPLIQUÉ STITCH

The appliqué stitch is used in this book to attach a piece of fabric to another and gives the outline a clean embroidered edge. Adjust the setting on your sewing machine so that the width of the stitch is narrow and the length short; I used a 3mm width and 1.5mm length on my machine.

ZIGZAG STITCH

Another decorative stitch that has various uses, the zigzag can be used in the same way as the appliqué stitch, or as a simple decoration, as I've done on the Llama's blanket (see page 56). Adjust the stitch width and length setting appropriate to the use.

SATIN STITCHES – STRAIGHT, TRIANGLE AND OVAL

These stitches are used for the faces in the Unicorn (see page 120), Spider (see page 108) and Llama (see page 56) projects. They are not essential but if your sewing machine has these options then this is a great opportunity to use them. Similar to the other decorative stitches you will want to keep the width and length of the stitch narrow and short to create a continuous strong line or shape – practise on scraps of fabric first. When you want to create an eye or the fang of the spider, for example, and if your machine allows it, use a single satin stitch or sew slowly to create an oval or triangle satin stitch.

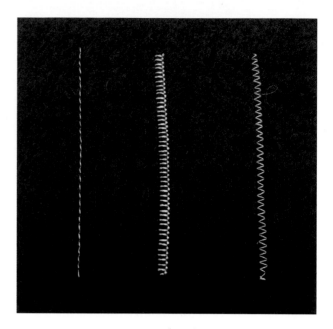

(L-R) RUNNING, APPLIQUÉ AND ZIGZAG STITCHES

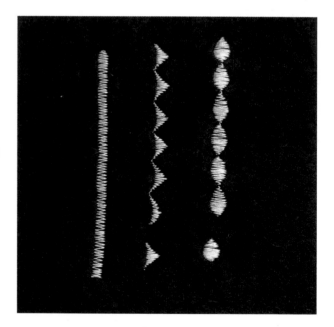

(L-R) STRAIGHT, TRIANGLE AND OVAL
SATIN STITCHES

DECORATIVE HAND STITCHES

There are two decorative hand stitches that have been used in some of the projects in this book: the running stitch and the seed stitch. Both are created using embroidery thread and can be tweaked to create texture, patterns or facial features.

RUNNING STITCH

This is a basic stitch that can be used along a straight or curved line. It has been used in the Kiwi Fruit project (see page 34) when attaching the stem to the skin.

Cut an 11¾in (30cm) length of embroidery floss and thread one end through an embroidery needle and then knot the other end. Start by bringing the needle up through the back of the fabric to the front, pulling the thread all the way through until the knot meets the underside of the fabric. Decide the length of the stitch needed and push the needle down from the front to the back. Pull the thread all the way through once more and then repeat the process, creating even-sized stitches spaced at regular intervals until you reach the finish point.

SEED STITCH

The seed stitch is a small, straight stitch, which is created in the same way as the running stitch, but rather than being sewn in a straight line, it is sewn in random directions with varying stitch lengths. This stitch was used to decorate the pepperoni on the Pizza Slice (see page 80), and for the eyelashes and mouths of the Sloth (see page 102) and Llama (see page 56).

The seed stitch was also used to create the small arrow-like patterns on the Cacti project (see page 96), but in a more controlled way: one long seed stitch in the centre with two short ones on either side, stitched at an angle. If you have trouble imagining the arrow, draw the pattern on the felt with an water-soluble fabric marker pen first.

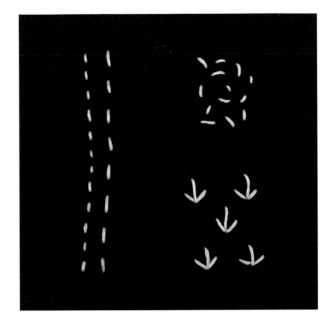

RUNNING (LEFT) AND SEED STITCHES

TIPS

Before starting any of the projects, spend time getting to know your sewing machine. Play around with stitch settings and what they can do by practising on spare pieces of fabric.

Embroidery thread is usually made of six strands. These can be separated before use, allowing you to control the thickness of the stitch when creating a decorative hand stitch.

SNOW-CAPPED MOUNTAIN

If you're looking for a quick and easy make, this snowy mountain is the peak of simplicity – an ideal project for your first plushie.

YOU'LL NEED:

Polar fleece fabric in grey – 3ft x 19¾in (1m x 50cm)

Dimple plush fabric in white – 4ft x 31½in (1.3m x 80cm)

Soft-toy filling

Sewing thread in grey and white

Sewing machine with ballpoint 90/14 stretch needle

Sewing needle

Pins

Fabric scissors

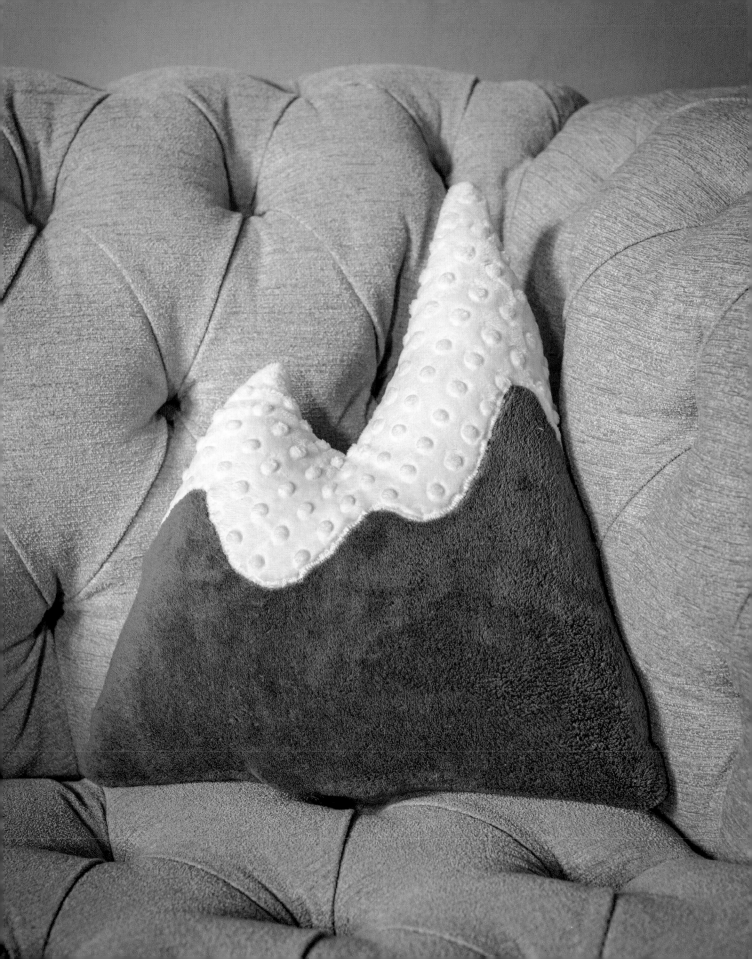

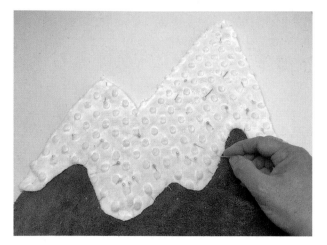

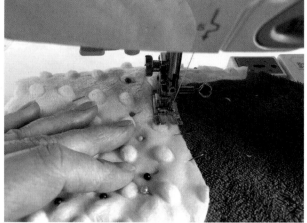

1 Fold the grey polar fleece fabric in half, right sides together, and using the Mountain template (see page 126), pin, cut out and put to one side. Fold the white dimple fabric in half, right sides together, and using the Snowcap template (see page 126), pin, cut out and put to one side. Take one grey mountain and place one of the white snowcaps over the top, with right sides facing up and ridges matching. Pin together, using plenty of pins to hold in place.

2 With the sewing machine set on a short, narrow appliqué stitch (see page 14) and using white thread, sew all the way along the base of the snowcap, backstitch (see page 12) either end and neaten off any stray threads. Repeat the same process with the other grey mountain and snowcap.

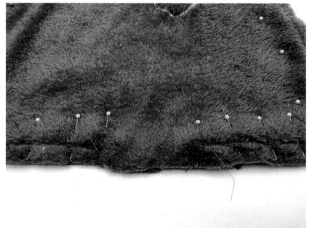

3 Place the mountain pieces right sides together so they match and pin all the way around the outer edges. Use plenty of pins to prevent the fabric from slipping.

4 Using a longer stitch setting on the sewing machine, sew a running stitch (see page 14) with a ½in (1.5cm) seam allowance all the way around the outer edge, stopping 2¼in (6cm) from where you started to leave a small gap. Backstitch either end and neaten off any stray threads with scissors.

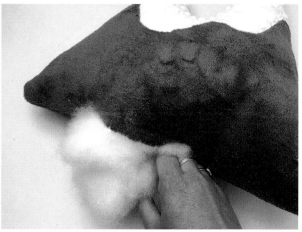

5 Trim the corners of the mountain with scissors and snip into the seam allowance around and in-between the mountain peaks.

6 Carefully turn the mountain right side out through the gap and use the rounded end of the scissors to carefully push out the pointed areas. Fill the mountain with the soft-toy stuffing until it is plump and all the peaks are firm.

7 With a sewing needle and grey thread, use invisible stitch (see page 12) to close the gap. Fasten off and trim any stray threads.

TIPS

To turn the mountain into a cushion cover, add a zip to the straight edge at the base.

Adapt the template to add more peaks to your mountain.

MONSTERA LEAF

Bring the outside in with this monstera (Swiss cheese) leaf – a great way to create that all-year-round urban jungle look indoors.

YOU'LL NEED:

Felt fabric in holly green – 19¾in (50cm) square

Dimple plush fabric in light green – 19¾in (50cm) square

Soft-toy filling

Sewing thread in green

Sewing machine with ballpoint 90/14 stretch needle

Sewing needle

Pins

Fabric scissors

Pencil

1 Place the felt fabric on top of the plush fabric with right sides facing. Using the Monstera Leaf template (see page 127), pin and cut out. Remove the template. Pin the two pieces of fabric together, right sides facing. Use plenty of pins to prevent the fabric from slipping.

2 Starting at the top of the leaf, with the sewing machine set on a longer stitch setting, sew a running stitch (see page 14) with a ½in (1.5cm) seam allowance around the outer edge of the leaf. Take your time and follow the shape of the leaf.

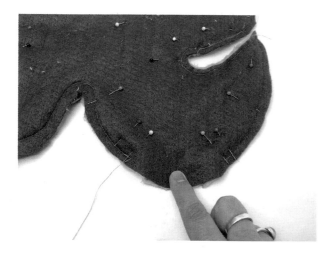

3 Stop sewing 2¼in (6cm) from where you started, leaving a gap for turning out the leaf. Remember to backstitch (see page 12) either end and trim any stray threads with scissors.

4 Snip into the seam allowance around the curved edges, then turn the leaf right side out through the gap. Run your finger along the inside seam to create a crisp edge and push out any pointed bits with the rounded end of a pencil.

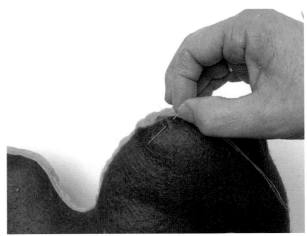

5 Fill the leaf with plenty of toy stuffing, paying particular attention to the tips.

6 With the sewing needle and green thread, use invisible stitch (see page 12) to close the gap. Fasten off and trim any stray threads.

TIPS

If you lightly fill the leaf with toy stuffing you can oversew the veins of the leaf to give it a quilted effect.

Create an assortment of autumn foliage by drawing simple paper templates and choosing a variety of autumnal-coloured fabrics.

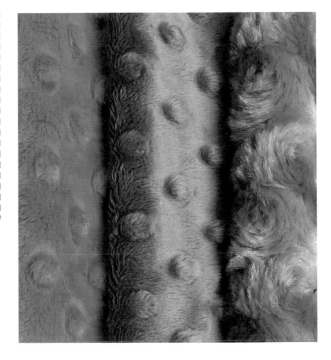

AVOCADO

Popular in salads, sandwiches and dips, the trendy avocado also makes the perfect cuddling companion. Here's how to create your own soft and huggable avocado.

YOU'LL NEED:

Smooth plush fabric in jade green – 13³/₄ x 9³/₄in (35 x 25cm)

Dimple plush fabric in brown – 13³/₄ x 11³/₄in (35 x 30cm)

Felt fabric in chestnut brown – 4³/₄in (12cm) square

Soft-toy filling

Sewing thread in brown

Sewing machine with ballpoint 90/14 stretch needle

Sewing needle

Pins

Fabric scissors

Pencil

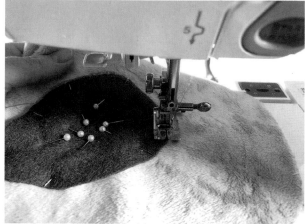

1 Using the Avocado templates (see page 128), pin and cut one Avocado Flesh from the green smooth plush fabric, two Avocado Skin pieces from the brown dimple plush fabric, and one Avocado Stone from the chestnut-brown felt fabric. Pin the felt stone to the front of the smooth plush flesh so that it sits in the centre. Make sure you use a few pins to prevent the fabric from slipping.

2 With the sewing machine set on a short and narrow appliqué stitch (see page 14), sew all the way around the outer edge of the stone. When you reach where you started, backstitch (see page 12), trim any stray threads with scissors, then put to one side.

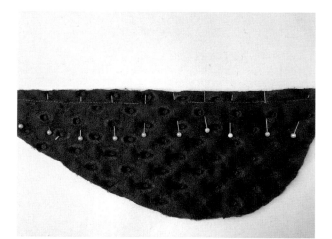

3 Pin the brown dimple plush fabric pieces right sides together so that the pins hold the straight edges securely. Then, using a longer stitch setting on the sewing machine, sew a running stitch (see page 14) along the straight edge with a ½in (1.5cm) seam allowance. Stop sewing after 4in (10cm) then backstitch. Leave a gap of about 3in (8cm) then continue sewing in running stitch until you reach the end, remembering to backstitch either end. This will be the turning-out gap.

4 For the stem, cut a 1½in (4cm) square piece of the chestnut-brown felt fabric. Fold it in half and carefully sew along three sides, rounding the top end and leaving the bottom edge open. Use a pencil to turn the stem the right side out.

5 With the avocado flesh facing up, place the stem at the top with its raw edge sitting just over the edge, then place the avocado skin, right sides facing, on top and pin all the way around the edge.

6 Using the sewing machine, sew a running stitch with a ½in (1.5cm) seam allowance all the way around, taking care not to let the fabric slip. Trim any stray threads then, with a sharp pair of scissors, snip into the seam allowance at regular intervals. Turn the avocado the right way out through the hole made in Step 3. Run your fingers along the inside seam to give a crisp edge.

7 Stuff the avocado with plenty of toy filling so that the shape becomes nice and plump. With a sewing needle and thread, use an invisible stitch (see page 12) to close the hole on the back of the avocado. Trim any stray threads.

TIPS

Adapt the template to create similar shaped fruits and vegetables, such as pears and aubergines.

Use the satin stitch on your sewing machine to sew a face on the avocado stone.

WATERMELON

A slice of fun, this fluffy pink and green watermelon is just waiting to be cuddled. Once you've mastered the melon, you can use the pattern to make a variety of fruits.

YOU'LL NEED:

Polyester fleece fabric in pink – 15¾ x 11¾in (40 x 30cm)

Felt fabric in black – 12in (30.5cm) square

Polar fleece fabric in white – 15¾in (40cm) square

Faux fur fabric in grass green – 23⅝ x 7¾in (60 x 20cm)

Soft-toy filling

Sewing thread in white, black and green

Sewing machine with ballpoint 90/14 stretch needle

Sewing needle

Pins

Fabric scissors

7 With the sewing machine set on the longer stitch setting and green thread, sew a running stitch along the pinned edge with a ½in (1.5cm) seam allowance and backstitch either end.

8 Pin the other side of the skin to the remaining watermelon edge then, using the same stitch setting, sew a running stitch with a ½in (1.5cm) seam allowance for about 9¾in (25cm) then stop and backstitch. Leave a gap of about 2¼in (6cm) and continue sewing in running stitch until you reach the end, remembering to backstitch either end. Trim and neaten off any stray threads.

9 Turn the watermelon the right way out through the gap then run your fingers along the inside seams to create a crisp edge. Fill with plenty of toy stuffng, paying particular attention to the corners.

10 Using an invisible stitch (see page 12), close the gap. Fasten off and trim any stray threads.

TIPS

You can use this template to create various pieces of sliced fruit or vegetable plushies.

Turn the watermelon into a cushion cover by inserting a zip along the straight edge.

KIWI FRUIT

With its tactile skin and soft, seeded centre, not only does this kiwi fruit make a great cushion, it's also a gentle reminder to eat your five a day.

YOU'LL NEED:

Faux lambswool fabric in brown – 23⅝ x 15¾in (60 x 40cm)

Felt fabric in lime green – 13¾ x 11¾in (35 x 30cm)

Polyester fleece fabric in white – 7¾ x 6in (20 x 15cm)

Felt fabric in black – 12in (30.5cm) square

Felt fabric in dark brown – 3in (8cm) square

Soft-toy filling

Sewing thread in brown, green, white and black

Embroidery thread in brown

Sewing machine with ballpoint 90/14 stretch needle

Sewing needle

Embroidery needle

Pins

Fabric scissors

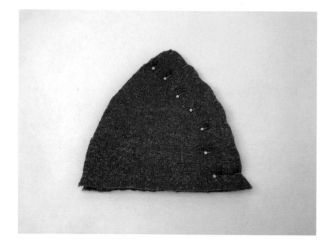

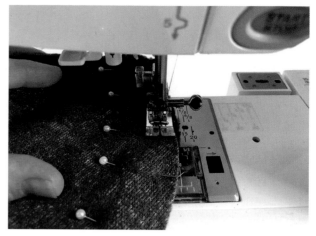

1 Using the Kiwi Fruit Skin template (see page 130), pin and cut out five pieces from the brown lambswool fabric. Take two of the fabric pieces and pin right sides together, down one of the curved edges.

2 With a longer stitch setting on the sewing machine and using brown thread, sew a running stitch (see page 14) with a ½in (1.5cm) seam allowance along the curved edge, remembering to backstitch (see page 12) either end. Repeat with the remaining kiwi skin pieces, attaching them one by one, then join the last piece to the first piece so that they form the back of the kiwi. Trim any stray threads and put to one side.

3 Using the Kiwi Fruit Flesh and Centre templates (see page 130), cut the flesh from the green felt fabric and the centre from the white fleece fabric. Pin the white fleece centre, fluffy side up, to the middle of the green kiwi flesh. With the sewing machine set on a short narrow appliqué stitch (see page 14) and using green thread, sew around the outer edge of the white centre. Neaten off any stray threads to the reverse.

4 Using the sewing machine and the same green thread, sew various running stitch lines from the edge of the white centre to the outer edge of the green flesh. Vary the length of the lines then repeat with the white thread. Neaten off any stray threads to the reverse of the flesh.

5 Using the Kiwi Seed templates (see page 130), cut out six large and five small from the black felt fabric. Position them around the white centre and pin in place. Then, using the same appliqué stitch (see Step 3) and black thread, carefully sew around the outer edge of each black seed. When all of the seeds have been attached, hand sew the stray threads through to the reverse and neaten off.

6 Pin together the kiwi skin and flesh, right sides together, making sure you use plenty of pins all the way around the outer edge.

TIPS

Use a soft plush green fabric for the flesh to create an extra cuddly kiwi fruit.

Adapt this pattern for other exotic fruits, such as papaya or dragon fruit.

7 Starting at the bottom of the kiwi and using brown thread, sew a running stitch with a ½in (1.5cm) seam allowance all the way around the outer edge. Stop sewing 2¼in (6cm) from where you started to leave a gap for turning out the kiwi. Remember to backstitch either end and trim any stray threads.

8 Using a pair of scissors, snip into the seams around the edge then turn the kiwi right side out through the gap. Run your finger along the inside seam to create a crisp edge and then fill the kiwi with plenty of toy stuffng.

9 Using the sewing needle and brown thread, use an invisible stitch (see page 12) to close the gap. Fasten off and trim any stray threads.

10 Using the Kiwi Stem template (see page 130), pin and cut out from the brown felt fabric. Position it in the centre on the back of the kiwi skin and pin in place. Using the embroidery needle and brown thread, hand sew a decorative running stitch (see page 15) through the stem to the skin in a circle. Fasten the thread off behind the stem.

LEMON

With its zing of vibrant yellow, this fluffy lemon is perfect for squeezing. Bright and cheery, it's just as happy on the kitchen table as on the sofa, and will add a drop of sunshine to any room.

YOU'LL NEED:

Shaggy plush fabric in yellow – 23⅝ x 11¾in (60 x 30cm)

Thick felt fabric in green – 12in (30.5cm) square

Thick felt fabric in brown – 4in (10cm) square

Soft-toy filling

Sewing thread in yellow, brown and green

Embroidery thread in brown

Sewing machine with ballpoint 90/14 stretch needle

Sewing needle

Embroidery needle

Pins

Fabric scissors

Pinking shears

1 Using the Lemon template (see page 130), pin and cut four lemon shapes from the yellow shaggy plush fabric. Take two of the pieces and place them right sides together, making sure the pointed ends match, then pin all the way down one curved edge.

2 With a longer stitch setting on the sewing machine and yellow thread, sew a running stitch (see page 14) with a ½in (1.5cm) seam allowance along the pinned edge. Backstitch (see page 12) either end and trim any stray threads.

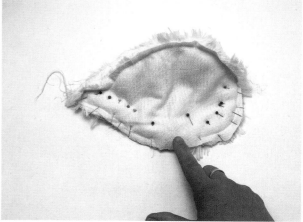

3 Attach the last two lemon pieces using the same process. Remember to sew as close to the pointed ends as possible and trim off any stray threads.

4 Join the first piece with the last piece by sewing along the edge as in the previous steps, but this time stop sewing after 3in (8cm) and backstitch. Leave a 2¼in (6cm) gap and start sewing again, remembering to backstitch at either end. (This will be the turning-out gap.) Put the lemon to one side.

5 Fold the green felt fabric in half and pin the Lemon Leaf template (see page 130) to it so that the tip is on the fold. Cut out the leaf shape, giving you two leaves, joined at the tip.

6 With the sewing machine and green thread, sew a running stitch down the centre of one leaf, branching off at various points to create the veins. Trim any stray threads. Repeat the same process with the other leaf.

7 Cut a circle, roughly measuring 3in (8cm) in diameter, out of the brown felt fabric with the pinking shears and place it over the point where the leaves are joined. Then, with the embroidery needle and brown embroidery thread, knot one end and sew a loose running stitch around the edge of the circle, going through the leaves. Pull on the thread so that the circle gathers slightly, fasten off on the reverse and put to one side.

8 Turn the lemon the right side out through the gap and stuff with toy filling. Using invisible stitch (see page 12), close the gap with the sewing needle and yellow thread. Fasten off and trim any stray threads. Position the leaves on top of the lemon. With a sewing needle and brown thread, and using invisible stitch again, carefully hand sew just under the brown circle to attach the leaves to the lemon. Fasten off and trim any stray threads.

AC

Let nature be your guid
acorn plushie! Once yo
squirrel away an

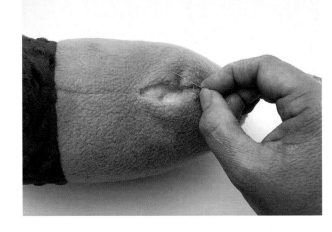

7 Turn the acorn right side out through the gap and stuff it with toy filling. With the sewing needle and brown thread, use invisible stitch (see page 12) to close the gap. Fasten off and trim any stray thread.

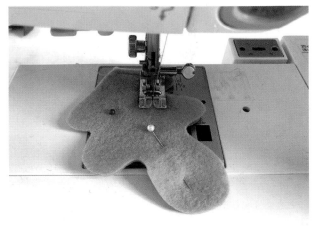

8 Using the Acorn Leaf template (see page 131), cut out two leaves from the lime green felt fabric and two from the holly green felt fabric. Pin the two lime leaves together and, using the sewing machine with green thread, sew a running stitch close to the edge, all the way around the leaf.

9 Sew a running stitch down the centre of the leaf, branching off at various points to create veins. Trim any stray threads, then repeat the process for the holly green leaf.

10 To attach the leaves to the top of the acorn, use the sewing needle and green thread to hand sew through one of the leaves, into the acorn top and then back through the leaf. Sew through the next leaf so that it sits at an angle over the first, then back through the first leaf to the acorn top. Fasten off behind the leaves and trim any stray threads.

WHALE

Make a splash with this super-cool sea dweller.
When she's not floating effortlessly through the blue,
this majestic marine creature is perfectly content
with lounging around.

YOU'LL NEED:

Felt fabric in midnight blue – 23⅝in (60cm) square

Dimple plush fabric in charcoal grey – 15¾ x 13¾in (40 x 35cm)

Soft-toy filling

2 round four-hole buttons in grey – ½in (1.5cm)
in diameter

Sewing thread in dark blue and grey

Embroidery thread in white

Sewing machine with ballpoint 90/14 stretch needle

Sewing needle

Embroidery needle

Pins

Fabric scissors

Pinking shears

Water/air-soluble fabric marker pen in white

Iron and ironing board

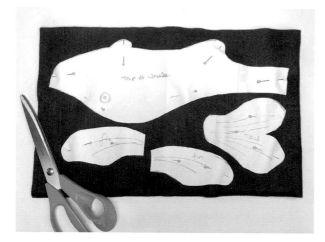

1 Fold the blue felt fabric in half. Using the Whale Upper Body, Tail and Fin templates (see page 132), pin to the felt fabric and, using pinking shears, cut out and put to one side. Repeat with the charcoal dimple plush fabric and the Whale Lower Body template (see page 132), making sure you use plenty of pins to secure and prevent the fabric from slipping.

2 Take the tail pieces of felt and pin together with right sides facing. Using the sewing machine and dark blue thread, and starting at the thin end of the tail, sew a running stitch (see page 14) with a ⅜in (1cm) seam allowance all the way around, leaving the flat, straight end open. Remember to backstitch (see page 12) at either end.

3 Repeat Step 2 with the two fins, remembering not to sew the flat, straight end as this will be where you turn the piece right side out later. Once the tail and the two fins have been sewn, snip around the curved edges with a pair of sharp scissors then turn each one right side out. Give them a light press with a warm iron.

4 Next, add some texture to the tail and fins. Using the sewing machine, sew a couple of lines of running stitch on each fin and at least four on the tail, following the curves. Trim any stray threads and put to one side.

5 Take the two upper body pieces and, with right sides facing, pin along the top. Then, using the sewing machine, sew a running stitch with a $\frac{3}{8}$in (1cm) seam allowance along the top part of the body only, starting at the tip of the nose and finishing at the tail end, remembering to backstitch either end. Snip into the seam allowance around the curved edges with scissors.

6 Turn the body piece right side out. Then, taking the two fins made earlier, pin them either side of the body so that they sit pointing up towards the first pointed ridge at the top of the body and with the raw edges of the fins aligned with the cut edge of the body. Next, flatten out the tail end of the body and pin the tail in place with the raw edges together. Then, using the sewing machine, sew a running stitch at the base of each one where the raw edges meet and put it to one side.

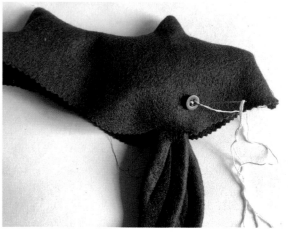

7 Take the two lower body pieces, place right sides together and pin along the base, making sure you use plenty of pins to prevent the fabric from moving when sewing. Then, with the sewing machine and grey thread, sew a running stitch for about 7¾in (20cm) along the base, with a ⅜in (1cm) seam allowance, starting at the tail end and remembering to backstitch either end. Leave a gap of about 2in (5cm) – this will become the opening for stuffing the whale – then continue sewing until you reach the mouth tip and backstitch. Trim any stray threads and put to one side.

8 To create the eyes, make a mark with the fabric marker pen on the inside of the upper body piece, as shown on the template. Using the embroidery thread and needle, with the thread knotted at one end, sew from the inside, then place the button where you came through and sew a cross through the four holes of the button. Make sure the button is secure, then fasten off on the inside. Repeat for the other eye.

9 Flatten out each of the body pieces and place on top of each other with right sides together. Pin all the way around, making sure the tail and fins are tucked inside. Then, with the sewing machine, sew a running stitch with a ⅜in (1cm) seam allowance all the way around, paying careful attention when going over the thicker areas. Once you have reached where you started, backstitch and fasten off any stray threads.

10 To turn the whale out to the right side, carefully push the tail end through the 2in (5cm) gap created in Step 7. The rest of the body should then pull through easily. Run your finger along the inside seam to push out any little dents.

11 Grab a small handful of toy filling and start filling the whale through the gap, making sure the small pointed tips of the body and the tail end have been fully filled.

12 Once the whale has been stuffed, use invisible stitch (see page 12) to close the gap with the sewing needle and grey thread. Fasten off and trim any stray threads with scissors.

TIPS

Pay attention to the direction of the nap when cutting out the dimple plush fabric – make sure it is going the same direction on any adjacent pieces.

If you prefer – or you're making this ocean dweller for a child (see page 10) – you can use felt circles instead of buttons for the eyes.

LLAMA

It's carnival time! With a colourful pom-pom crown, decorative stitching and cheeky face, this lovable llama is ready to party. Create a happy herd in a variety of bright colours.

YOU'LL NEED:

Felt fabric in mushroom, pale pink, lime green and bright pink – 12in (30.5cm) square

Smooth plush fabric in natural – 15¾in (40cm) square

Soft-toy filling

Pom-poms in various colours and sizes

Sewing thread in cream, pale pink, lime green, white and black, plus contrasting colours

Sewing machine with ballpoint 90/14 stretch needle

Sewing needle

Pins

Fabric scissors

Pinking shears

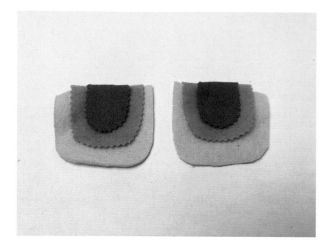

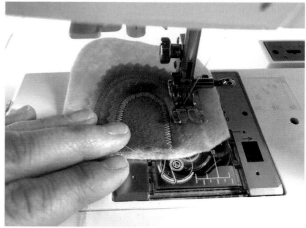

1 Using the Llama Blanket 1 template (see page 133) and fabric scissors, pin and cut out two from the pale-pink felt fabric. Using the Llama Blanket 2 (see page 133) and pinking shears, pin and cut out two from the lime-green felt fabric. Using the Llama Blanket 3 template (see page 133) and pinking shears, pin and cut out two from the bright-pink felt fabric. Place them on top of each other in order of size, to give you two sets, and pin in place.

2 With the sewing machine set on a short, narrow appliqué stitch (see page 14) and using threads in contrasting colours to the felt, sew ¼in (5mm) in from the edge around the top and middle layers of felt. Backstitch (see page 12) either end. Repeat for the other blanket set.

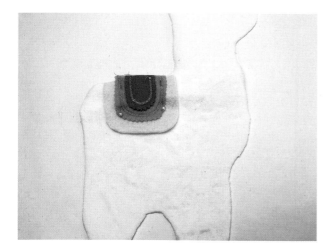

3 Fold the natural plush fabric in half. Using the Llama Body template (see page 133), pin and cut out to give you two pieces. Take one piece of the body fabric and pin one of the blanket sets to it, so that the straight edge matches the straight edge of the llama's back. Repeat with the other llama body piece and blanket set.

4 Using the same appliqué stitch (see Step 2) and green thread, carefully sew around the outer edge of the blanket on each of the pieces of llama body to attach. Backstitch at either end and trim any stray threads.

5 Using the Llama Ear template (see page 133), pin and cut out two from the natural plush fabric and two from the mushroom felt fabric. Take one of each and pin right sides together to make a matching pair. Then take one pair and, with the sewing machine and white thread, sew a running stitch (see page 14) with a ⅜in (1cm) seam allowance all the way around the curved edge, leaving the straight edge open. Backstitch at either end. Turn the ear right side out then, with the sewing needle and cream thread, hand sew the straight edge together to create a pinch. Repeat with the other ear.

6 Using the Llama Face template (see page 133), pin and cut out one piece from the mushroom felt fabric. With the sewing machine set on the narrow, straight decorative satin stitch (see page 14) and using black thread, sew a mouth and nose in the centre of the face. (If your sewing machine does not have this setting, see page 61 for an alternative.)

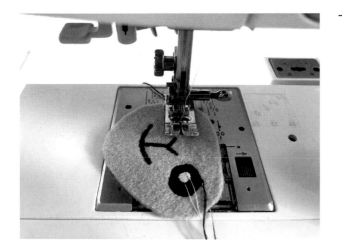

7 For the eyes, cut out two small black felt circles and sew around the outer edges with the same stitch and black thread. Change the thread to white and sew a small oval decorative satin stitch in the centre of each eye. Hand sew any loose threads to the reverse and fasten off. Sew some eyelashes above the eyes using an embroidery needle and black embroidery thread.

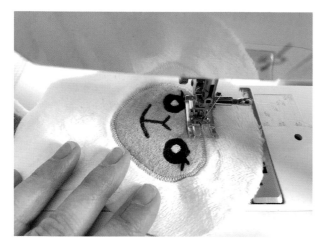

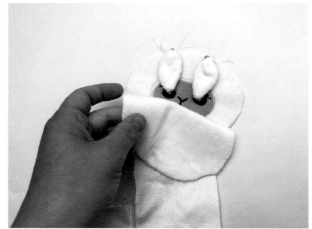

8 Pin the face to the front of the head on one of the llama body pieces and carefully sew around the outer edge, using the same appliqué stitch (see Step 2) with cream thread. Backstitch either end.

9 With the piece of llama body fabric that has the face attached facing up, place the ears at the top with the raw edges sitting just over the edge. Then place the other piece of llama body fabric on top, right sides together, and pin through both pieces of fabric to secure the ears in place. Make sure the edges of the blankets match up, then pin all the way around the llama.

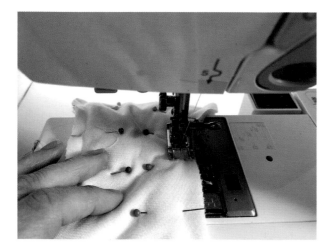

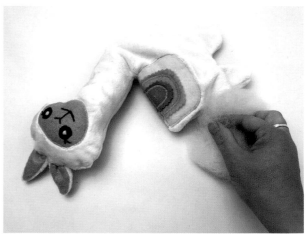

10 Using the sewing machine on a longer stitch setting, sew a running stitch with a 1/2in (1.5cm) seam allowance all the way around the outer edge, starting from above the llama's back leg. Make sure you sew through all the layers, stopping 2in (5cm) from where you started, and backstitch either end.

11 Remove the pins. Using a pair of scissors, snip into the seam allowances around the curved edges. Turn the llama the right side out through the gap. Fill the llama body with toy stuffing, paying particular attention to its long neck and head.

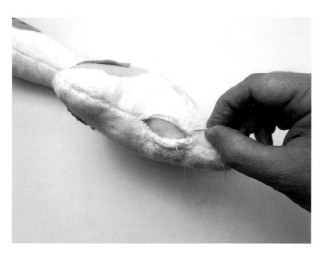 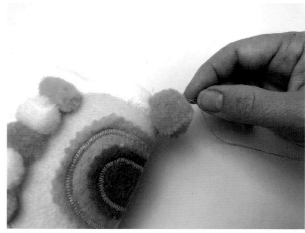

12 Using the sewing needle and cream thread, use invisible stitch (see page 12) to close the gap. Fasten off and trim any stray threads.

13 All llamas need a bit of decoration, so using various colours and sizes of pom-poms, hand sew a few between the ears for a pom-pom crown, some along the bottom of the blanket, and then sew on a larger one at the rear of the llama for a tail. Trim any stray threads.

TIPS

If your sewing machine doesn't have decorative stitch settings, use felt circles for the eyes and hand sew a mouth in seed stitch (see page 15), using embroidery thread.

Make a herd of llamas using different coloured fabrics, various types of pom-pom, and other decorative trimmings.

ICED DOUGHNUT

When you find yourself reaching for another one of those doughnuts from the bakery, settle down to create this guilt-free option instead.

YOU'LL NEED:

Felt fabric in sand brown – 3ft (1m) square

Dimple plush fabric in lemon yellow – 19¾in (50cm) square

Soft-toy filling

Pom-poms in various colours and sizes

Sewing thread in beige, pale yellow and white

Sewing machine with ballpoint 90/14 stretch needle

Sewing needle

Pins

Fabric scissors

Tracing paper

Water/air-soluble fabric marker pen

Pencil

String

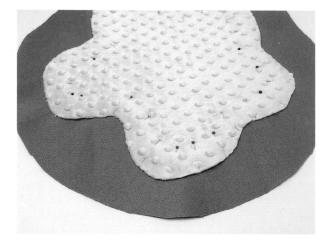

1 Cut two circles from the tracing paper – one measuring 17³/₄in (45cm) in diameter, the other with a 4³/₄in (12cm) diameter (see Tip, page 66). Using the larger circle template, pin and cut out two circles from the sand felt fabric and put them to one side. Then make a freehand drawing of the shape of the icing on the large circle template, so that it fits within the circle, and cut out. Pin the icing template to the reverse of the lemon dimple fabric and cut out. Next, take one of the large felt fabric circles and, with right sides facing up, place the lemon icing fabric on top and pin, using plenty of pins to hold the icing in place.

2 With the sewing machine set on a short, narrow appliqué stitch (see page 14) and using yellow thread, sew all the way around the outer edge of the icing. Backstitch (see page 12) either end and neaten off any stray threads.

3 Place both of the large felt fabric circles right sides together and pin. Then position the small circle template in the centre and trace the shape using the fabric marker pen. Remove the template and pin the area.

4 With the sewing machine set on a longer stitch setting and using the beige thread, sew a running stitch (see page 14) directly onto the circle you drew and backstitch either end. Then cut the doughnut hole out, leaving a ½in (1.5cm) seam allowance. Carefully snip into the seam allowance along the curved edge with the scissors.

5 Turn the doughnut right side out by pulling from the centre, then gently flatten with your hands so that the edges meet.

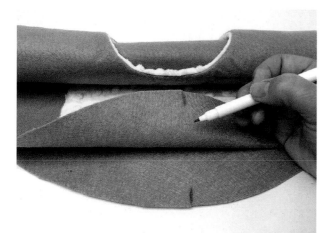

6 Using the fabric marker pen, draw a line on the icing side and one on the other circle directly underneath, so that the two marks match. Roll the opposite side of the doughnut in on itself to the centre.

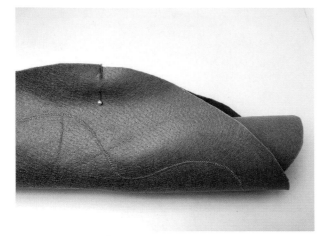

7 Bring the marked edges of the circle up around the rolled part, so that the marks are now right sides together, and pin.

8 Using the sewing machine, start sewing a running stitch around the outer curve of the circle with a 1/2in (1.5cm) seam allowance. When you reach the bottom of the curve, stop sewing. Keep the presser foot and needle down and gently pull out the fabric from inside the doughnut, making sure to match the pieces right side to right side. Continue to sew around the doughnut, but stop sewing 2 1/4in (6cm) from where you started to leave a gap. Backstitch either end.

9 Pull the doughnut right side out through the gap and fill with toy stuffing. Use invisible stitch (see page 12) to close the gap with sewing needle and thread. Fasten off and trim any stray threads.

TIPS

To create your doughnut-shaped templates, tie a piece of string to a pencil to help you draw a perfect circle. The string should measure the radius of your circle once tied to the pencil.

If you don't have pom-poms, use bright scraps of fabric for the sprinkles instead.

10 Using the needle and thread, hand sew on a variety of coloured pom-poms to create the doughnut sprinkles. Sew through a pom-pom then through to the lemon icing layer a few times and fasten off just under the pom-pom to hide the thread. Repeat with the other pom-poms.

SUSHI

Feed your takeaway craving with these fun, oversized versions of your favourite Japanese creations. They make the perfect gift for sushi lovers, too.

YOU'LL NEED:

Polyester fleece fabric in pink – 19¾ x 13¾in (50 x 35cm)

Dimple plush fabric in dusty pink – 13¾ x 9¾in (35 x 25cm)

Polyester fleece fabric in white – 27½ x 23⅝in (70 x 60cm)

Felt fabric in black – 25½ x 6in (65 x 15cm)

Dimple plush fabric in pumpkin orange – 7¾ x 4in (20 x 10cm)

Faux fur in black – 29½ x 7¾in (75 x 20cm)

Soft-toy filling

Sew-on Velcro – 3½in (9cm) in length

Sewing thread in white, pink, orange and black

Sewing machine with ballpoint 90/14 stretch needle

Sewing needle

Pins

Fabric scissors

1 **To make the fish sushi:** using the Sushi Fish template (see page 134), pin and cut two pieces from the pink fleece and pin together so that the right sides are visible. With the sewing machine set on a longer running stitch (see page 14) and using pink thread, carefully sew the chevron pattern of lines shown on the template. Start by sewing the first part of the centre line and then continue, sewing the lines branching off as you go. Neaten any stray threads.

2 Lightly fill the chevron pockets created in Step 1 with some of the toy filling, including the tail and head ends. Try not to fill too close to the edges.

3 Using the Sushi Fish template again (see page 134), cut one piece from the dusty-pink dimple plush fabric and pin right sides together to the fleece fish. Make sure you use plenty of pins to secure all the way around the outer edge.

TIPS

When creating the chevron pattern on the fish, use pins to mark out the lines as a guide.

Change the colour of the square to green for an avocado sushi filling.

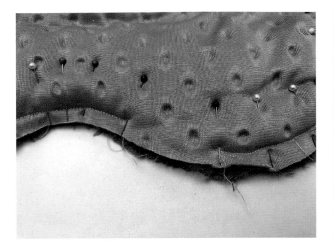

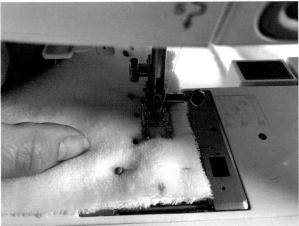

4 Using the sewing machine set on a long running stitch, sew all the way around the outer edge, stopping 2¼in (6cm) from where you started. Backstitch (see page 12) either end and trim any stray threads. Turn the fish right side out through the gap and stuff with the toy filling. Then, using the sewing needle and pink thread, close the gap using invisible stitch (see page 12). Fasten off and trim any stray threads. Put to one side.

5 To make the rice, take the white fleece fabric and cut a length measuring 4 x 21¼in (10 x 54cm). Using the wrong side of the fleece as the right side (to give the rice a more fluffy texture), fold the strip in half, with the short raw edges meeting and the fluffy side on the inside. Pin in place and then, using the sewing machine and white thread, sew a running stitch with a ½in (1.5cm) seam allowance along the short edge so that the strip forms a loop. Backstitch either end and trim any stray threads.

6 Using the Sushi Rice Rectangle template (see page 135), pin and cut two pieces from the white fleece fabric. Take one piece, remembering to use the wrong (fluffy) side as the right side, and pin the loop around the outer edge, right sides together. Using the sewing machine, sew a running stitch all the way around the outer edge, remembering to backstitch either end.

7 Pin the remaining sushi rice piece to the other side of the loop and, with the sewing machine and white thread, sew a running stitch all the way around, stopping 2¼in (6cm) from where you started to create a gap. Backstitch either end then pull the sushi rice rectangle right side out through the gap. Stuff with toy filling. Using invisible stitch (see page 12), close the gap with sewing needle and thread. Fasten off and trim any stray threads.

8 To make the seaweed wrap, cut a strip of black felt fabric, measuring 24½ x 4in (62 x 10cm), using pinking shears. Peel the Velcro apart, pin one side to the end of the felt and, using the sewing machine with black thread, sew a running stitch around the edge of the Velcro. Wrap the strip around the fish and rice as a guide for positioning the other piece of Velcro. Pin in place, then sew in the same way. Wrap around the fish and rice, and fasten.

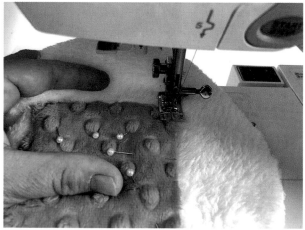

9 **To make the sushi roll:** pin and cut out two pieces of white fleece using the Sushi Rice Circle template (see page 135). Using the Sushi Salmon Square template (see page 134), cut out two pieces from the orange dimple plush fabric. Take one circle, with the wrong (fluffy) side facing up, and pin the salmon square in the centre.

10 Using the sewing machine set on a short, narrow appliqué stitch (see page 14) and using orange thread, sew all the way around the outer edge of the square. Backstitch either end. Neaten off any stray threads and repeat with the remaining circle and square.

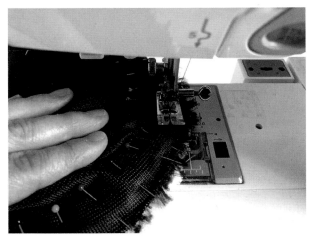

11 Cut a length of the black fur fabric measuring 26¾ x 6in (68 x 15cm) for the outer seaweed loop. Fold one of the shorter ends over by ½in (1.5cm) to form a seam and pin one corner to the outer edge of the sushi rice circle, right sides together. Then continue to pin the length of black fur fabric all the way around the outer edge until it overlaps where you started. You'll need to use plenty of pins.

12 With the sewing machine set on a longer running stitch, sew all the way around the pinned circle, taking care that the fabric underneath does not curl. Backstitch either end then pin and sew the remaining circle to the other side of the black seaweed loop in the same way. Remember to fold the other end of the seam first.

13 Turn the sushi roll the right side out through the seam gap on the seaweed loop that was not sewn and fill with the toy stuffing. Make sure you push plenty of filling in to accentuate the shape.

14 Using the sewing needle and black thread, close the gap with invisible stitch. Fasten off and trim any stray threads.

PEAS IN A POD

Plump and sweet, these cute little plushie peas are ready to pop from their furry pod. Give them some 'pea-sonality' by sewing on smiley faces.

YOU'LL NEED:

Smooth plush fabric in jade green – 23⅝ x 17¾in (60 x 45cm)

Faux fur fabric in grass green – 15¾in (40cm) square

⅛in- (3mm-) thick felt fabric in lime green – 15¾in (40cm) square

Soft-toy filling

Sewing thread in green

Sewing machine with ballpoint 90/14 stretch needle

Sewing needle

Pins

Fabric scissors

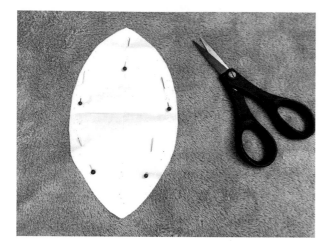

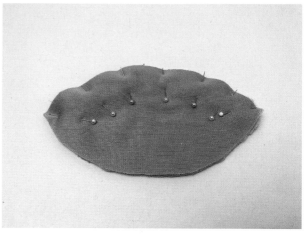

1 Using the Pea template (see page 136), pin and cut out 12 pieces from the jade-green plush fabric. Take four of the pieces and put the rest to one side.

2 Take two of the pea pieces and place them right sides together, making sure the pointed ends match, then pin all the way down one curved edge.

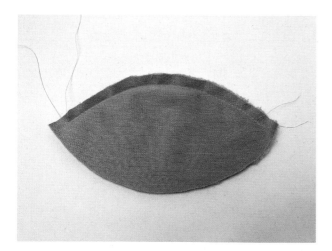

3 With a longer stitch setting on the sewing machine and using green thread, sew a running stitch (see page 14) with a ½in (1.5cm) seam allowance along the pinned edge, leaving the tips unsewn. Backstitch (see page 12) either end and trim any stray threads with scissors.

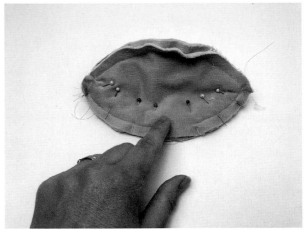

4 Attach the other two pea pieces using the same method, remembering to backstitch either end and trim off any stray threads.

5 Join the first piece with the last piece by sewing along the edge as in the previous steps, but stop after 1¼in (3cm) and backstitch. Leave a ¾in (2cm) gap and start sewing again, remembering to backstitch either end. (This will be the turning-out gap.)

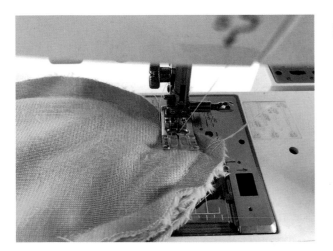

6 Using the sewing machine, sew across all the layers at each end where the points meet – this will give the pea shape its roundness. Then, with the scissors, snip into the seam allowance along the curved edges.

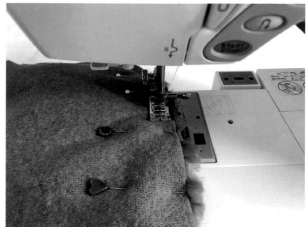

7 Turn the pea right side out and fill with plenty of toy filling. Use invisible stitch (see page 12) to close the gap with the sewing needle and green thread. Fasten off and trim any stray threads. Repeat Steps 2–7 to create two more peas using the remaining jade-green pieces of fabric cut out in Step 1.

8 Using the Pea Pod template (see page 136), cut out two from the faux fur fabric and two from the felt fabric. Take the two fur pieces and pin right sides together. Using a longer stitch setting on the sewing machine and green thread, sew a running stitch with a ½in (1.5cm) seam allowance along the curved edge, leaving the straight edge unsewn. Backstitch either end, then put to one side.

9 Repeat with the two green felt pieces, remembering to backstitch either end. Snip into the curved part of the seam allowance on both pod pieces with a pair of scissors and then place the fur pod inside the felt pod, right sides together. Pin all the way around the top straight edge of the pod to hold the two pieces in position.

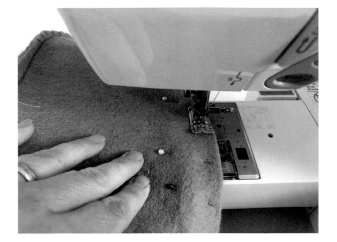

10 Carefully sew a running stitch with a ½in (1.5cm) seam allowance along the straight edge of the pod, stopping 2¼in (6cm) before where you started to leave a small gap. Backstitch either end and trim any stray threads with the scissors.

11 Turn the pod right side out through the gap, then push the green felt part of the pod inwards so that the green fur becomes the outside of the pod. Use invisible stitch to close the gap with the sewing needle and green thread. Fasten off and trim any stray threads. To complete the project, simply place the three peas inside the pod!

TIPS

When you cut the faux fur fabric, give it a good shake before sewing to release any loose fibres.

Use a different textured fabric for the lining of the pod for a variation.

Add character to the peas by sewing on smiley faces using a decorative hand stitch (see page 15).

PIZZA SLICE

Melted cheese, spicy pepperoni and rich tomato sauce on a soft, fluffy crust – sounds delicious, doesn't it? Here's how to add a slice of Italy to your home. And the best part? There's no washing-up!

YOU'LL NEED:

Polar fleece fabric in yellow – 11¾in (30cm) square

Smooth plush fabric in light brown – 19¾ x 11¾in (50 x 30cm)

Felt fabric in tomato red – 11¾in (30cm) square

Felt fabric in burgundy – 12in (30.5cm) square

Soft-toy filling

Sewing thread in yellow, brown and burgundy

Embroidery thread in beige and ruby

Sewing machine with ballpoint 90/14 stretch needle

Sewing needle

Embroidery needle

Pins

Fabric scissors

Water/air-soluble fabric marker pen

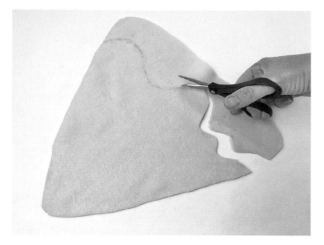

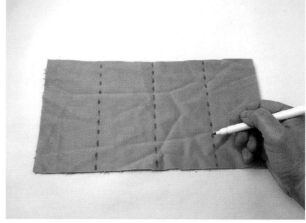

1 Using the Pizza template (see page 137), pin and cut out one from the yellow fleece, one from the red felt and one from the brown plush fabric. Take the yellow fleece piece and on the reverse, using a fabric marker pen, draw a rough squiggly line along the top edge to give the effect of melted cheese. Cut along the line and put to one side with the other pizza fabric pieces.

2 Using the Pizza Crust template (see page 137), pin and cut out from the brown plush fabric. Using the fabric marker pen, mark the reverse of the fabric with three vertical lines, evenly spaced along the length of the crust, to create four sections.

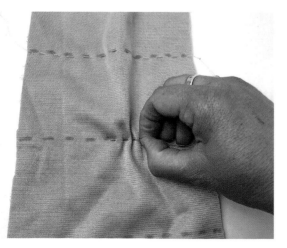

3 Using the sewing needle and brown thread, hand sew a loose running stitch (see page 15) along the first drawn line. Do not tie off the ends and leave at least 4in (10cm) of thread loose at either end. Repeat for the remaining two lines.

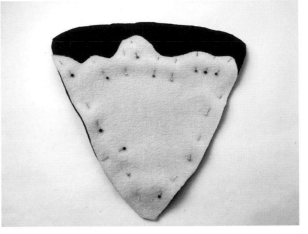

4 Fold the pizza crust fabric in half lengthways, right sides together, and pin in place. With the sewing machine set on a longer stitch setting, sew a running stitch (see page 14) with a ½in (1.5cm) seam allowance along the short straight edges, remembering to backstitch (see page 12) either end. Then turn the crust right side out and gently pull on the loose threads to create a ruched effect. Knot each of the threads to keep the ruche in place, then fill each pocket with a little of the toy filling and put to one side.

5 Take the red felt pizza piece of fabric and place the yellow fleece layer on top with the fluffy side facing up. Using plenty of pins, secure the two pieces together.

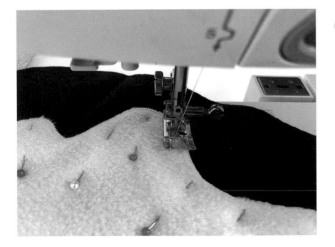

6 With the sewing machine set on a short narrow appliqué stitch (see page 14) and using yellow thread, sew along the squiggly edge of the yellow fleece fabric to attach it to the red felt pizza piece. Then, using a running stitch on the sewing machine, sew along the remaining straight edges of the yellow fleece.

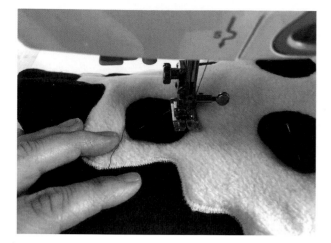

7 Using the Pizza Pepperoni template (see page 137), pin and cut six pieces from the burgundy felt fabric. Place each one randomly on the yellow fleece part of the pizza with a couple hanging over the edge. Then, using the same narrow appliqué stitch (see Step 6) and the burgundy thread, sew around the outer edge of each one to secure in place and neaten off any stray threads to the reverse of the fabric. For the detail on the pepperoni, take the embroidery needle and beige embroidery thread and, using seed stitch (see page 15), sew small lines in different directions and lengths to create a textured effect. Repeat with the ruby thread. Fasten off and trim any stray threads.

8 Lay the brown plush piece of pizza fabric on the table, right side facing up, then position the pizza crust along the top of the plush pizza piece with the raw edges matching. Then place the pizza topping piece on top, right sides together, and pin all the way around the edge.

TIPS

Add more toppings to your pizza slice, such as mushrooms or olives, by cutting out and sewing on other colourful felt pieces.

Make a few more slices and add Velcro to the sides to form a whole pizza.

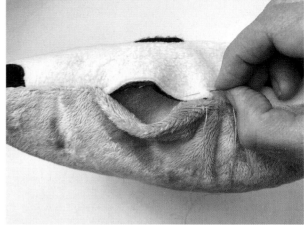

9 Using the sewing machine, start sewing a running stitch with a ½in (1.5cm) seam allowance all the way around the outer edge of the pizza, stopping 2¼in (6cm) before where you started to leave a small gap. Backstitch either end and trim off any stray threads. Turn the pizza right side out through the gap. Fill with toy stuffing.

10 Use invisible stitch (see page 12) to close the gap with the sewing needle and brown thread. Fasten off and trim any stray threads.

TOADSTOOL

Everyone loves fairy-tale toadstools with their iconic red hats and white spots. Create a few, but make sure you don't overfill them as there might not be 'mush-room'!

YOU'LL NEED:

Smooth plush fabric in red – 19¾in (50cm) square

Felt fabric in white – 13¾in (35cm) square

Soft-toy filling

Sewing thread in white and red

Sewing machine with ballpoint 90/14 stretch needle

Sewing needle

Pins

Fabric scissors

Pinking shears

Water/air-soluble fabric marker pen (optional)

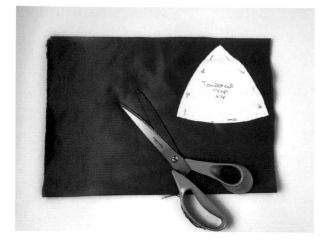

1 Pin the Toadstool Stem, Stem Base, Cap Base and Spots templates (see page 138) onto the white felt fabric and cut out, using pinking shears for the outer edge of the cap base and fabric scissors for everything else. Repeat with the Toadstool Cap template and the red plush fabric, using pins or a fabric marker pen to mark the points that will form the top of the toadstool.

2 Take two of the red cap pieces and pin right sides together down one edge, matching the top points together. With the sewing machine on a longer stitch setting and red thread, sew a running stitch (see page 14) with a ½in (1.5cm) seam allowance and backstitch (see page 12) either end. Put to one side and repeat the process with the remaining two cap pieces so that you end up with two sewn halves. Next, pin the two halves right sides together, making sure the seams match at the top, and sew a running stitch along that edge with a ½in (1.5cm) seam allowance. Remember to backstitch either end. Trim any stray threads.

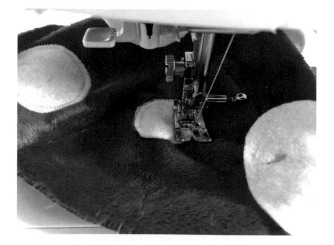

3 Once the toadstool cap has been made, turn it right side out and position the white felt spots on top in random places, with some hanging over the edge. Pin into position. When you are happy with their position, set the sewing machine on a short, narrow appliqué stitch (see page 14) and, using white thread, sew all the way around the outer edge of each white spot. Trim any stray threads.

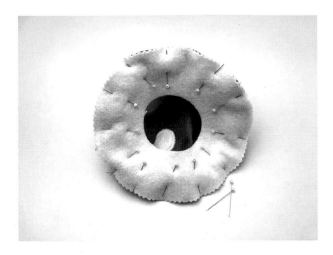

4 Turn the cap inside out and pin the felt cap base to the inner edges. Using the sewing machine and white thread, sew a running stitch around the edge with a ½in (1.5cm) seam allowance and backstitch either end. Trim any stray threads. Snip into the seam allowance around the outer edge. Turn the toadstool right side out and stuff with toy filling until it's firm, then put to one side.

5 To create the stem of the toadstool, fold the white felt stem piece in half lengthways and use the sewing machine to sew a running stitch along the straight edge with a ½in (1.5cm) seam allowance to create a tube. Backstitch either end. Position the wider end of the tube onto the white felt base and pin all the way around to hold in place. Sew a running stitch around the edge with a ½in (1.5cm) seam allowance. Backstitch either end and then snip around the outer edge with a pair of scissors. Turn the stem right side out and run your fingers around the inside of the seam to give a clean edge. Trim any stray threads. Fill the stem with toy filling, making sure it's plump and firm.

6 Join the stem to the base of the cap with invisible stitch (see page 12), using a sewing needle and white thread. Before closing the gap completely, add a bit more toy filling to plump up the area then finish hand sewing to close.

TIPS

Add gills to the toadstool cap base by hand sewing running stitches with embroidery thread.

Use different-coloured plush fabrics to create a selection of autumnal toadstools.

PUMPKIN

Straight from the pages of a storybook, this beautiful pumpkin has all the hallmarks of the magical, horse-drawn version. You'll have to wait until nightfall to see if you've weaved a magic spell.

YOU'LL NEED:

Smooth plush fabric in orange – 29½ x 19¾in (75 x 50cm)

Felt fabric in dark green and chestnut brown – 12in (30.5cm) square

Soft-toy filling

Sewing thread in orange, brown and green

Embroidery thread in green

Sewing machine with ballpoint 90/14 stretch needle

Sewing needle

Embroidery needle

Pins

Fabric scissors

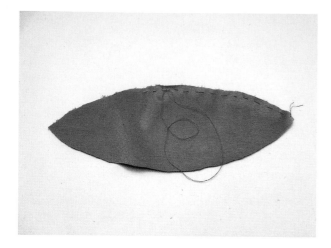

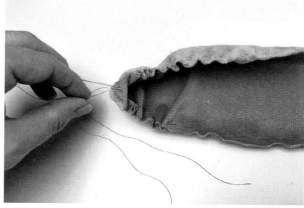

1 Using the Pumpkin templates (see page 139), pin and cut out seven Pumpkin Panels from the orange smooth plush fabric, two Large and two Small Pumpkin Leaves from the dark-green felt fabric, and two Pumpkin Stems and one Pumpkin Base from the chestnut-brown felt fabric. Take one of the panels and, using the sewing needle and orange thread, tie a knot at one end and hand sew a loose, wide running stitch (see page 15) down one side, about ⅜in (1cm) from the edge. Once you have reached the end, do not tie a knot, but remove the needle and leave about 4in (10cm) of thread. Repeat the process on the other side of the panel with both knots at the same end. Put it to one side and repeat with the remaining panels.

2 Take one of the panels and carefully pull both threads with one hand while holding the knotted end with the other. The sides will start to gather. Continue to pull the threads while spreading out the gathers so that the panel shrinks to about 6in (15cm) in length. Knot the thread ends together and repeat the process with the remaining panels.

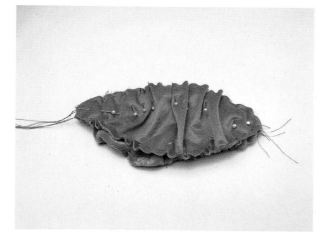

3 Take two of the panels, right sides together, and carefully pin down one side. Using a longer stitch setting on the sewing machine, sew a running stitch (see page 14) with a ½in (1.5cm) seam allowance along that edge, sewing over the gathered edges. Remember to backstitch (see page 12) either end.

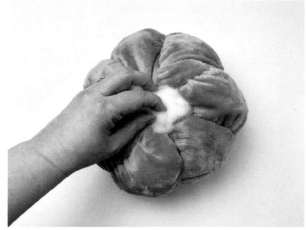

4 Take another panel, pin it to the two you have already sewn together, and then sew it using the same technique used in Step 3. Repeat the process with the remaining panels until you have attached them all. It will become more difficult to sew as you add more panels, so make sure you pin them carefully.

5 You should be left with a large opening. Pin the two sides of the opening together then sew, stopping 2in (5cm) from the top to leave a gap. Give all the long threads a slight pull, tie them together then trim with scissors. Turn the pumpkin right way out through the gap and fill with toy filling. Make sure you use plenty of stuffing to plump up the pumpkin. Using the sewing needle and thread, close the gap with invisible stitch (see page 12) and trim any stray threads. Put the pumpkin to one side.

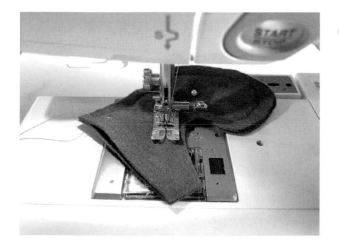

6 To create the stem, pin the two pieces of felt together and, using the sewing machine, sew a running stitch with a $3/8$in (1cm) seam allowance all the way around, leaving the straight edge open. Backstitch either end. Snip any curved edges of the seam allowance with scissors and turn the whole thing right side out. Use the rounded end of the scissors to push any difficult areas out, then stuff the stem with toy filling.

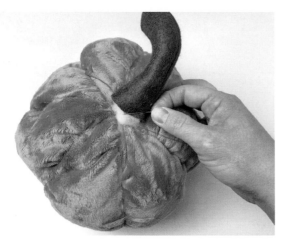

7 Place the base of the stem on top of the pumpkin, deciding how you want it to sit, then with a sewing needle and brown thread, and using invisible stitch, carefully hand sew the stem onto the pumpkin. Trim any stray threads.

8 For the pumpkin base, take the felt circle and, using the sewing needle and brown thread knotted at one end, sew a loose running stitch all the way around, as close to the edge as possible. Then, gently pull the thread so that it gathers the edges to the centre of the circle, creating a smaller, puffier decorative circle. With the thread still attached to the puff, use invisible stitch to sew the piece to the bottom of the pumpkin with the detailed side facing up.

TIPS

Try using a dimple-textured plush fabric for a knobbly pumpkin effect.

If you find the gathered effect too difficult to achieve, then leave those steps out – your pumpkin will be just as handsome.

9 To create the leaves, pin together the two larger felt leaves and, using the sewing machine and green thread, sew a running stitch all the way around the leaf, close to the edge. Then sew down the centre of the leaf, branching off at various points to create the veins. Trim any stray threads. Repeat the process for the smaller leaf.

10 To connect the leaves to the pumpkin, using the green embroidery thread and needle, sew through the big leaf at the top of the central vein. Then, keeping the thread on the needle, sew through the base of the stem on the pumpkin. Allow the leaf to hang from the stem then tie a knot in the thread to keep it in position. Trim any stray threads. Repeat with the remaining leaf so that it sits slightly higher and overlaps the larger leaf.

CACTI

Add a pop of colour to the room with a spike-free cactus plushie... or three! As low maintenance as plants get, you can sit this trio on a shelf or cosy up to them in an armchair.

YOU'LL NEED:

Dimple plush fabric in cactus green and olive green – 29½ x 19¾in (75 x 50cm)

Felt fabric in holly green – 3ft x 19¾in (1m x 50cm)

Felt fabric in yellow, red, fuchsia and pink – 12in (30.5cm) square

Shaggy plush fabric in yellow – 2¼in (6cm) square

Soft-toy filling

Sewing thread in green

Embroidery thread in green – 3 skeins of 26ft (8m)

Embroidery thread in orange – 1 skein of 26ft (8m)

Sewing machine with ballpoint 90/14 stretch needle

Sewing needle

Embroidery needle

Pins

Pinking shears

Fabric scissors

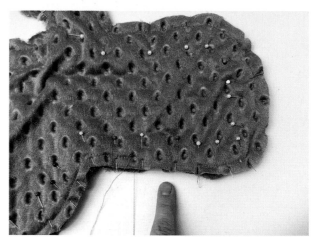

1 **To make the tall cactus:** fold the cactus-green dimple fabric in half, right sides together. Using the Tall Cactus template (see page 140), pin to the fabric and cut out. Remove the template then re-pin the pieces together, using plenty of pins around the outer edge.

2 Using the sewing machine on a longer stitch setting and green thread, sew a running stitch (see page 14) with a ½in (1.5cm) seam allowance all the way around the cactus, stopping 2in (5cm) from where you started. Backstitch (see page 12) either end.

3 Snip into all the curved parts of the seam allowance with scissors and turn the cactus right side out through the gap. Stuff the cactus with the toy filling until it is nice and firm, paying particular attention to the thinner parts. Then, use invisible stitch (see page 12) to close the gap.

4 **To make the short cactus:** repeat Steps 1–3 using the olive-green plush fabric and the Short Cactus template (see page 141).

5 **To make the felt cactus:** use the Felt Cactus template (see page 141) to cut out 12 pieces from the holly-green felt and put to one side. Take two of the felt pieces and pin together around the scalloped edge. Using the sewing machine, sew a running stitch with a ½in (1.5cm) seam allowance around the scalloped edge only, remembering to backstitch either end. Repeat the process with the remaining felt pieces so that you end up with six sewn scalloped pieces. Trim any stray threads.

6 Using the scissors, snip into the seam allowance along the curves, then turn each one right side out, pushing out the scallops carefully with the rounded end of the scissors.

TIPS

Instead of flowers, why not sew some colourful mini pom-poms around the edges.

If the tips of the felt cactus don't quite meet, hand sew them together and cover the joins with the flower.

---

7 With the embroidery needle and green embroidery thread, use seed stitch (see page 15) to hand sew little arrows onto each side of the felt pieces, keeping them simple and leaving space around each one. You can keep the thread on the needle as you go from arrow to arrow, but remember to put a knot in the thread when finishing or starting a new piece. Once all six pieces have been embroidered, turn them inside out and put to one side.

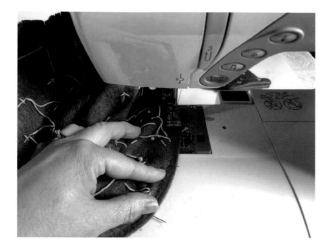

8 To bring the felt cactus together, take two of the felt pieces and pin right sides together along one straight edge, making sure they are both the right way up. Then, using the sewing machine, sew a running stitch with a ½in (1.5cm) seam allowance along the straight edge, remembering to backstitch either end.

9 Repeat the process with the remaining felt pieces until you are left with a large gap where the last two straight sides need to meet. Pin these together then sew along the edge as before, but stop sewing after 4in (10cm) and backstitch. Leave a 2in (5cm) gap and start sewing again, remembering to backstitch either end. Turn the cactus right side out through the gap and use the rounded end of the scissors to push out the scalloped features. Fill the cactus with plenty of toy filling and use invisible stitch to close the gap.

10 **To make the flowers:** Once the cacti have been made, you can start to add some flower details. First, using the Flower Petals templates (see pages 140–141), cut out two per cactus, using different shapes and coloured felts. Take two of the petals and place one on top of the other, then, using a sewing needle and thread, sew in the middle to hold in place. Repeat with the remaining petals.

11 To create the centre of each flower, use the following technique or those in Steps 12 and 13. Fold in half a piece of yellow felt that measures roughly 2¼ x 1½in (6 x 4cm). Using the pinking shears, cut into the fold at intervals of ⅜in (1cm) or so, stopping just before the edge, then carefully roll the felt widthways while still folded and, using the needle and thread, sew through the uncut end to hold in position. With the thread still attached, sew the centre to one of the flowers created in Step 10 and ruffle up the cut ends.

12 Another technique is to wind some orange embroidery thread several times around two fingers, then gently remove from your fingers and tie a piece of embroidery thread around the middle. While still holding the tied threads, cut through the loops and fluff up to form a small tassel. Sew the tied threads of the tassel to the centre of a flower.

13 The final technique has been used for the felt cactus. Cut a 2¼in (6cm) diameter circle from the yellow shaggy plush fabric. With the sewing needle and thread, sew a large running stitch (see page 15) around the edge. When you have reached the beginning, pull on the threads so that the circle gathers to the centre to form a fluffy ball. With the needle and thread still attached, tie a knot to secure then sew the ball to the centre of one of the flowers made in Step 10. Once all the flowers have been made, sew onto the cacti from the back of the flower using invisible stitch. Fasten off and trim any stray threads.

SLOTH

Take things slow with this furry creature. He may stretch your skills, but by the end of the project his sleepy eyes will lull you into those soft arms for a well-deserved rest.

YOU'LL NEED:

Felt fabric in mushroom and chestnut brown – 12in (30.5cm) square

Smooth plush fabric in brown – 31½ x 19¾in (80 x 50cm) square

Felt fabric in black and white – 4 x 2in (10 x 5cm)

Soft-toy filling

Sewing thread in brown, white and black

Embroidery thread in black

Sewing machine with ballpoint 90/14 stretch needle

Sewing needle

Embroidery needle

Pins

Fabric scissors

1 To make the claws, pin the Sloth Claw template (see page 142) onto the mushroom felt fabric and cut out eight to give you four pairs. Take one pair and, with right sides together, use the sewing machine with brown thread to sew a running stitch (see page 14) with a ⅜in (1cm) seam allowance all the way around the curved edge, leaving the straight edge open. Turn the claw right side out and then, using the sewing machine, sew two vertical lines to create the claw look, fasten off and trim any stray threads. Repeat with the remaining three pairs, then put to one side.

2 Using the Sloth Arm and Leg templates (see page 142), pin and cut four of each from the brown plush fabric. Take two leg pieces and place right sides together. Lift the rounded end of the top layer of fabric and place a claw within so that the raw edge of the claw just touches the edge of the leg. Replace the top layer and pin all the way around to hold in place. Repeat for the remaining leg and arms.

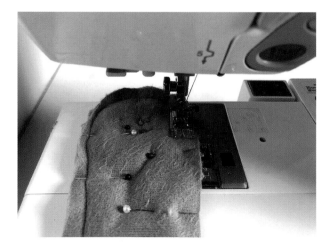

3 Take one of the legs and, with the sewing machine set on a longer stitch setting, sew a running stitch with a ⅜in (1cm) seam allowance all the way around, leaving the short, straight edge open. Snip around the outer edge of the curved end with a pair of scissors. Sew the remaining leg and arms in the same way then turn each one the right way out.

4 Once the legs and arms have been made, fill each one with some toy filling, but do not overfill them as you want them to be floppy (it will also make them easier to sew later), then put to one side.

5 Using the Sloth Face template (see page 142), pin and cut out from the mushroom felt fabric. Using the Sloth Eye Patch and Nose Patch templates (see page 142), pin and cut out two eye patches and one nose from the chestnut-brown felt fabric. Then, with the sewing machine set on a short, narrow appliqué stitch (see page 14), attach the eye patches and nose by sewing all the way around the outer edges.

6 Using the Sloth Nose template (see page 142), pin and cut out from the black felt. Cut out two white felt circles and two smaller black circles for the eyes. Using a sewing needle and matching thread, hand sew the nose and eyes over the patches sewn in Step 5. Fasten off and trim any stray threads. Then, using the embroidery needle and black thread, sew on a mouth using seed stitch (see page 15). Fasten off and trim any stray threads.

7 Using the Sloth Body template (see page 142), pin and cut out two pieces from the brown plush fabric. Position the felt face central to the head and pin in place. With the sewing machine set on the same appliqué stitch (see Step 5), carefully sew all the way around the outer edge of the felt face and neaten any stray threads.

8 The following steps will be tricky, so take your time. Place the body piece with the felt face attached to it on the table with the face facing upwards. Then take the two arms and position them so that they sit just below the head with the raw edges hanging over the edge of the body. (You'll find that if you cross the arms, one over the other, they will just fit.) Then take the other piece of body and place it on top, right side down, and pin the top half of the sloth, from just under the arms upwards.

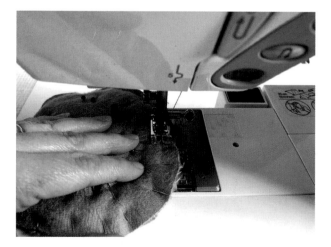

9 Using the sewing machine, carefully and slowly sew a running stitch with a ⅜in (1cm) seam allowance from just below the arm all the way around the pinned area, stopping just after the second arm and remembering to backstitch either end. Check that the arms are attached.

10 Once the top half has been sewn, push the arms up and out of the way into the head. Place the legs within the body so that the raw edges stick out and pin all the way around the lower half. Using the same running stitch and starting 3in (8cm) from where you stopped in Step 9, sew the lower half of the body, remembering to backstitch at either end. You should be left with a gap of 3in (8cm) on the side.

11 Remove the pins and turn the sloth right side out through the gap then stuff the sloth body with toy filling, making sure the rounded area of the head has plenty of filling.

12 Using invisible stitch (see page 12), close the gap, fasten off and trim any stray threads.

TIPS

If you have decorative stitch settings on your machine you can use them for the face instead of felt.

Sew slowly and carefully when attaching the arms and legs. Don't be afraid to check that they have been sewn on correctly before closing the gap.

SPIDER

How many spiders would you actually want to cuddle? With its cute, friendly face, this one might just change your mind. Don't be surprised if it gives unwary visitors a fright, though!

YOU'LL NEED:

Faux fur scale-effect fabric in black – 23⅝ x 19¾in (60 x 50cm)

Felt fabric in black – 11¾ x 7¾in (30 x 20cm)

Felt fabric in light grey – 12in (30.5cm) square

Soft-toy filling

Sewing thread in black and white

Sewing machine with ballpoint 90/14 stretch needle

Sewing needle

Pins

Fabric scissors

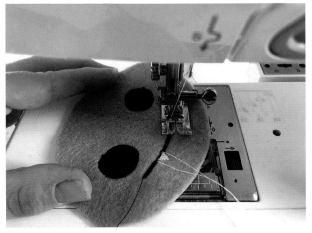

7 Using the Spider Back Base template (see page 143), pin and cut one from the black felt fabric. Open up the fur back made in Step 6 and pin the base, right sides together, to the felt back. Sew a running stitch around the curved edges, leaving the short, straight edge open. Turn the spider's back right side out and trim any stray threads. Put to one side.

8 Using the Spider Face template (see page 143), pin and cut one from the light-grey felt fabric. Cut two small black circles from the black felt for eyes. Position the eyes central to the face and, with the sewing machine set on a short, narrow appliqué stitch (see page 14) and using black thread, sew all the way around the outer edge of each eye. Then, using the narrow, straight decorative satin stitch (see page 14) on the sewing machine, sew a mouth directly below the eyes. For the fangs, change the thread to white and use a triangle satin stitch (if your sewing machine has one) for each fang, and an oval satin stitch in the centre of each eye. Hand sew any loose threads through to the reverse and fasten off.

TIPS

If your sewing machine doesn't have decorative stitch settings, use felt triangles for fangs and hand sew a mouth using embroidery thread.

You can use this pattern, minus the back part, to create an octopus!

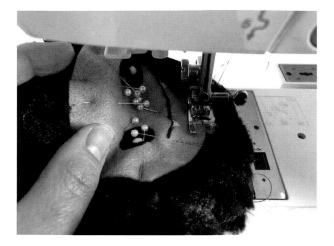

9 Pin the face to the front of the head (made in Step 2) and carefully sew around the outer edge using the appliqué stitch on the sewing machine. Use plenty of pins and take your time to prevent the felt face from slipping.

10 Pin the legs to the outer edge of the head so that they sit either side of the face and fix in place by sewing a running stitch. Then, using the Spider Head Base template (see page 143), cut one from the black felt fabric. Using a needle and black thread, hand stitch the base to the head using invisible stitch (see page 12). Before closing the gap, stuff the head with toy filling, then continue sewing to close the gap. Fasten off and trim any stray threads.

11 Fill the spider's back (made in Step 7) with the toy filling and, using invisible stitch, hand sew it onto the back of the spider's head with the textured surface facing up. Fasten off and trim any stray threads.

ANIMAL MASKS

Create an ark of wild animals with these fun masks. These fox, deer, giraffe and tiger masks are ideal for dressing-up and will keep the whole family entertained.

Felt fabric in earth brown, black, buttercream yellow, giraffe print, tiger print and white – 12in (30.5cm) square

Smooth plush fabric in natural/white – 11³/₄ x 9³/₄in (30 x 25cm)

Felt fabric in teddy brown – 23⁵/₈ x 17³/₄in (60 x 45cm)

Rose-swirl plush fabric in cappuccino brown – 6in (15cm) square

Dimple plush fabric in brown – 7³/₄ x 6in (20 x 15cm)

Polar fleece in camel brown – 4³/₄ x 4in (12 x 10cm)

Soft-toy filling

Elastic in black – ³/₄in (2cm) wide

Sewing thread in cream, black and brown

Sewing machine with ballpoint 90/14 stretch needle

Sewing needle

Pins

Fabric scissors

Water-soluble fabric marker pen

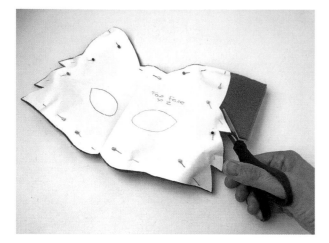

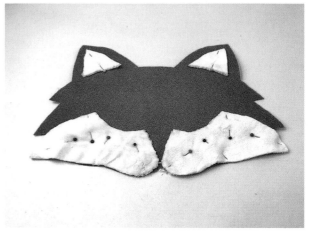

1 **To make the fox mask:** place the earth-brown felt fabric on top of the teddy-brown felt fabric. Pin the Fox Face template (see page 144) to both layers and then cut out with sharp scissors.

2 Using the Fox Whiskers and Fox Inner Ear templates (see page 144), pin and cut out two of each from the natural/white smooth plush fabric then pin them onto the earth-brown piece of felt fabric.

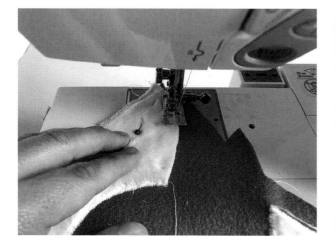

3 With the sewing machine set on a short, narrow appliqué stitch (see page 14) and using cream thread, sew all the way around the outer edge of the inner ears and the whiskers. Take it slowly around the bottom edge of the whiskers (if your sewing machine has an overlock stitch then use that on the bottom area of the whiskers). Fasten off and trim any stray threads.

4 Take the Fox Mask template (see Step 1) and place it over the mask you have just made. With the marker pen, draw where the eyes will sit, using the template as a guide. Using the Fox Eyebrow template (see page 144), cut out two from the natural smooth plush fabric and pin in place just above the drawn eyes. Fix them to the mask using the same appliqué stitch (see Step 3). Trim any stray threads.

5 Using the Fox Nose template (see page 144), pin and cut out one from the black felt fabric. Position it where the whiskers meet. Using the appliqué stitch with black thread, start sewing from one side, along the base of the nose, then stop sewing and fill the nose with a small amount of toy filling. Continue sewing along the top of the nose to where you started.

6 Once all the features have been sewn onto the mask, place it right side up over the plain teddy-brown felt piece cut out in Step 1. Pin together. Using the sewing machine and brown thread, sew over the eyes drawn in Step 4 with a running stitch (see page 14). Trim any stray threads between the two layers. With a sharp pair of scissors, cut out the centre of each eye.

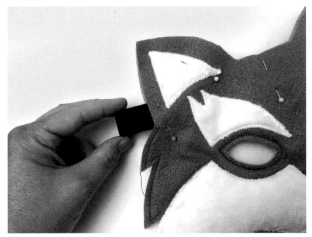

7 While the pins are still attached, sew a running stitch around the lower half of the mask to secure the two layers. Remove the pins then add a small amount of toy filling in between the layers where the whiskers are. Then, using the sewing machine, sew a running stitch around the top edge of the whiskers to enclose the toy filling. Neaten off the stray threads within the mask.

8 Cut a length of elastic approximately 11¾in (30cm) long. Place the raw ends of the elastic in between the two layers of felt and on either sides of the fox mask. Pin in place. Then, using the sewing machine, sew a running stitch around the rest of the mask, making sure you backstitch over the layers where the elastic sits and neaten off the stray threads.

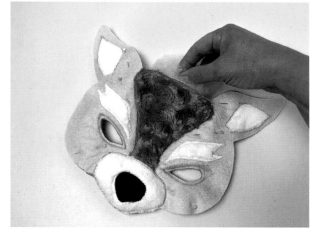

9 **To make the deer mask:** follow Steps 1–8, using the Deer Mask templates (see page 145). Use the buttercream felt fabric for the face and the cappuccino-brown plush fabric for the forehead. The only difference will be attaching the forehead before the muzzle, and remembering to add the toy filling to the forehead before sewing the outer edge of the mask.

10 **To make the giraffe mask:** follow Steps 1–8, using the Giraffe Mask templates (see page 146). Use the giraffe-print felt fabric for the main mask, the brown dimple plush fabric for the muzzle, and black felt fabric for the eyebrows. For the ossicones (antlers), which sit at the top of the giraffe's head, use the Giraffe Ossicone template (see page 146) to cut two pieces of the camel-brown fleece and two of the teddy-brown felt fabric. Take one of each and place them right sides together, then, using the sewing machine and brown thread, sew a running stitch with a ⅜in (1cm) seam allowance around the edge, leaving the bottom edge open. Repeat with the other pair. Snip into the seam allowance with scissors and turn them right side out.

TIPS

Check the length of elastic before attaching to see if it fits the head – you may need less.

Use a variety of textured fabric or patterned felt to create different animal masks.

11 Place the raw ends of the ossicones between the two layers of felt, just at the top of the head, and sew around the outer edge of the mask.

12 **To make the tiger mask:** follow Steps 1–8, using the Tiger Mask templates (see page 147). Use the tiger-print felt fabric for the main part of the mask and white felt for the fangs. Attach the fangs to the mask between the two layers of felt fabric when sewing the outer edge of the muzzle, before stuffing it with toy filling.

UNICORN

With its glittery mane and mythical horn, this plushie is a must-have for unicorn fans. Add some more sparkle with ribbons and jewels and it's sure to win Best in Show.

YOU'LL NEED:

Sparkle plush fabric in white/silver – 3ft x 25½in (1m x 65cm)

Dimple plush fabric in dusty pink – 7¾in (20cm) square

Felt fabric in yellow – 12in (30.5cm) square

Felt fabric in gold – 19¾ x 7¾in (50 x 20cm)

Soft-toy filling

Sewing thread in white, black, yellow and pale pink

Sewing machine with ballpoint 90/14 stretch needle

Sewing needle

Pins

Fabric scissors

Pinking shears

Tissue paper

Ruler

Water/air-soluble fabric marker pen

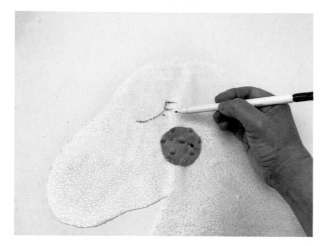

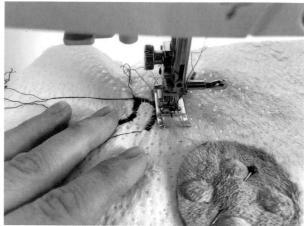

1 Using the Unicorn Head template (see page 148), pin and cut two pieces from the white sparkle plush fabric, then cut two 2¼in (6cm) diameter circles from the pink dimple fabric. With right sides up, place and pin a circle on each unicorn head for the cheeks and then, using the fabric marker pen, draw on the unicorn eyelashes.

2 Place a square piece of tissue paper (see page 13) behind one of the drawn eyelashes and, using the narrow, straight decorative satin stitch (see page 14) on the sewing machine and black thread, sew directly over the drawn lines. Take your time and try not to stretch the fabric. Tear the tissue paper away and trim any stray threads. Repeat with the other piece of unicorn head fabric.

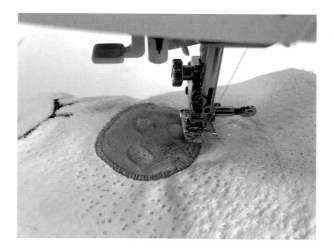

3 With the sewing machine set on a short, narrow appliqué stitch (see page 14) and pink thread, sew all the way around the outer edge of the pink cheek. Backstitch (see page 12) and trim any stray threads. Repeat with the other cheek and put the fabric pieces to one side.

4 | Using the Unicorn Ear template (see page 148), pin and cut two from the pink dimple fabric and two from the white sparkle fabric. Take one of each and pin right sides together. With the sewing machine set on a longer stitch setting, sew a running stitch (see page 14) with a ½in (1.5cm) seam allowance around the outer curved edge of the ear and backstitch either end. Repeat with the remaining pieces of ear fabric and then turn each one right side out.

5 | With a sewing needle and white thread, hand sew a loose running stitch (see page 15) along the bottom of each ear. Pull the thread to gather the fabric at the base and fasten off. Then position each ear above the cheek of the unicorn face, pointing downwards with the white sparkle side facing up and pin. Using the sewing machine, sew a running stitch across the gathered area and backstitch either end. Trim any stray threads.

6 | Using the Unicorn Horn template (see page 148), pin and cut two pieces of yellow felt fabric and pin right sides together. Then, using the sewing machine and yellow thread, sew a running stitch around the curved edges and backstitch either end. Turn the horn right side out and lightly fill with some of the toy filling. Sew a few lines of running stitch at an angle to create the spiral effect of the horn. Fasten off, trim any loose threads, then put to one side.

7 To create the unicorn's mane, cut two strips of gold felt fabric measuring x 17¼ x 2½in (44 x 7cm) with the pinking shears. Then, using the fabric marker pen, on the reverse of each strip make marks at intervals of ¾in (2cm) along the full length. Using the pinking shears, make cuts of at least 2in (5cm) into the strips at each mark.

8 Holding both strips wrong sides together, pin to one of the unicorn head pieces, starting from the base and working along the back of the head to the top. Bend and tweak the mane as you go, making sure the fringed part is facing into the unicorn face. Using the sewing machine, carefully sew along the straight edge with a ½in (1.5cm) seam allowance and backstitch either end.

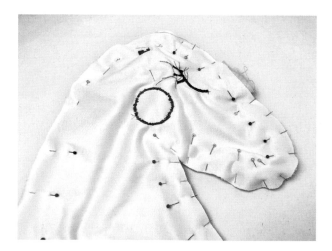

9 Place the horn at the top of the unicorn head, next to the end of the mane, with its raw edge sitting just over the edge. Then position the remaining piece of unicorn head fabric over the top, right sides together, and pin all the way around the edge.

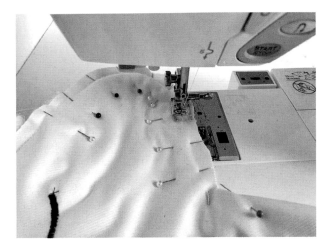

10 Starting from the base, with the sewing machine set on a longer stitch setting, sew a running stitch with a ½in (1.5cm) seam allowance around the outer edge of the unicorn, making sure you sew through all the layers carefully. Stop sewing 2¼in (6cm) from where you started to leave a gap, remembering to backstitch either end and trim any stray threads.

11 With a pair of scissors, snip into the seam allowance around the curved edges then turn the unicorn right side out through the gap. Fill the unicorn with toy filling, paying particular attention to the nose and corners. Next, close the gap with invisible stitch, (see page 12), using the sewing needle and white thread. Fasten off and trim any stray threads.

12 Using the sewing needle and pink thread, pin back the ear and sew through the pink part of the ear and into the unicorn head to hold it in position. Repeat for the other ear and trim any stray threads.

TIPS

Use embroidery thread to sew on the features if your sewing machine does not have decorative stitch settings.

Decorate the unicorn by creating felt flowers and sewing them onto the head.

TEMPLATES

SNOW-CAPPED MOUNTAIN
Page 16
Copy at 200%

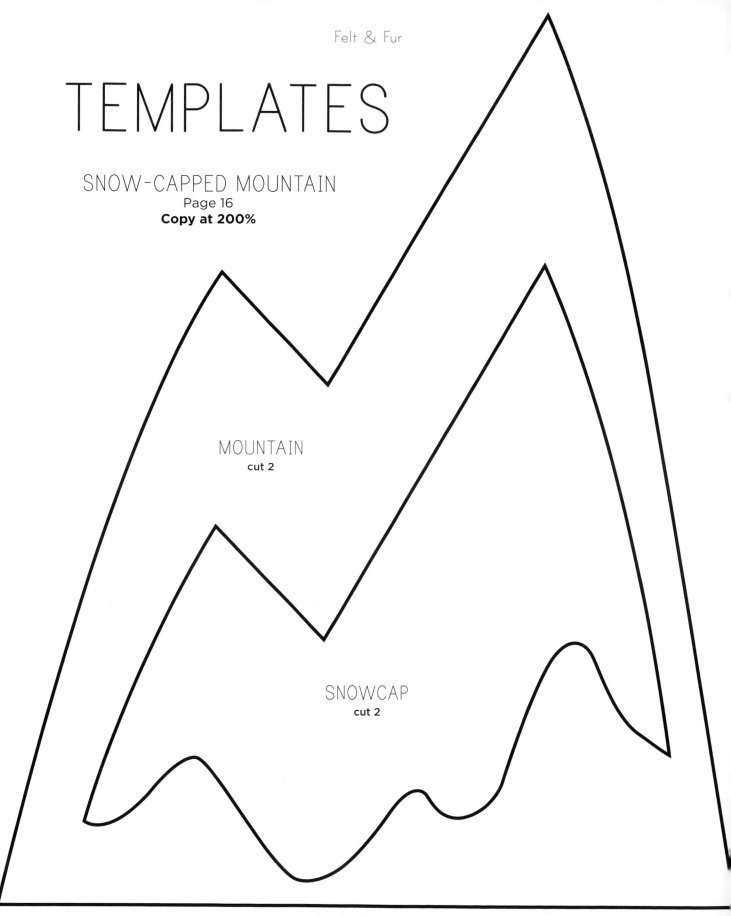

MOUNTAIN

cut 2

SNOWCAP

cut 2

MONSTERA LEAF
Page 20
Copy at 200%

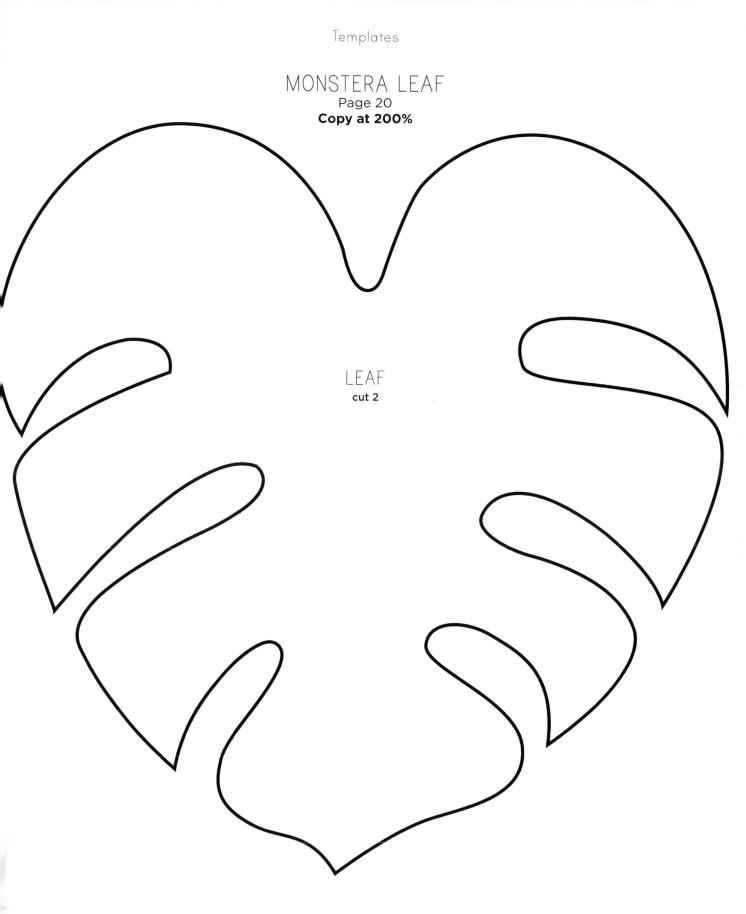

LEAF

cut 2

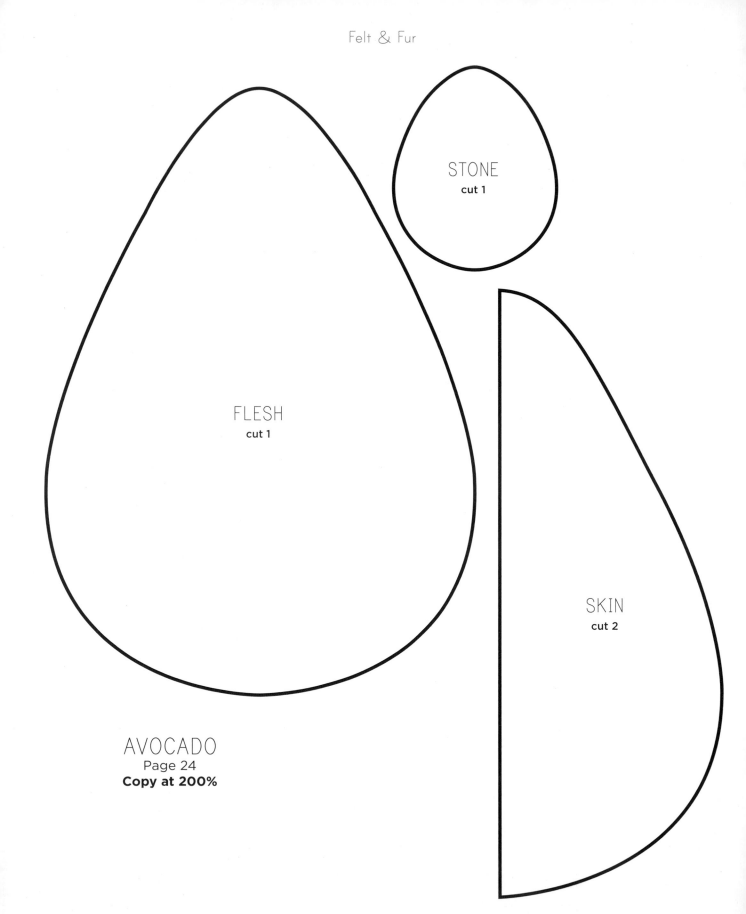

STONE
cut 1

FLESH
cut 1

SKIN
cut 2

AVOCADO
Page 24
Copy at 200%

WATERMELON
Page 28
Copy at 285%

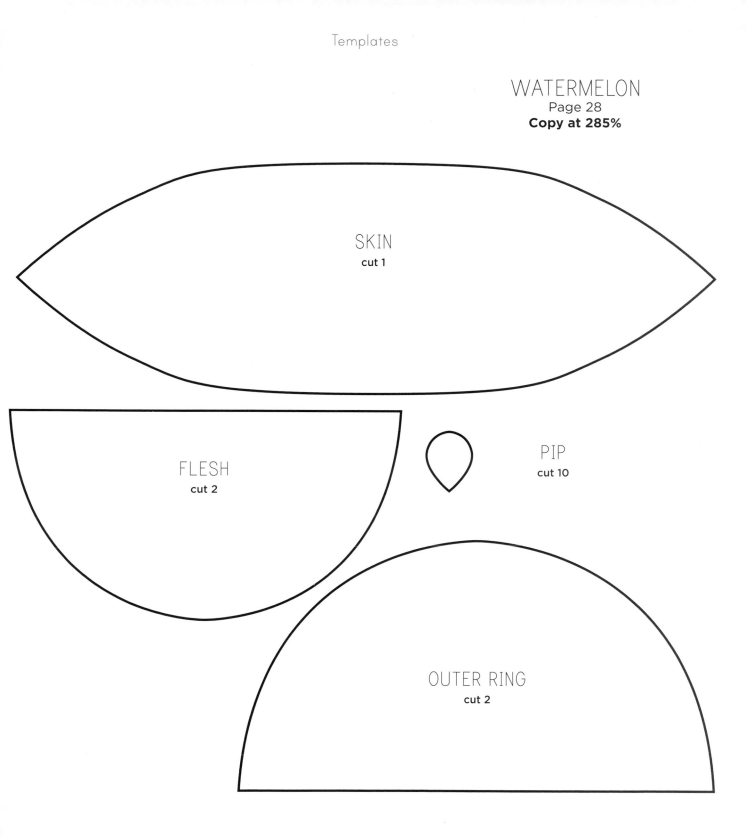

SKIN
cut 1

FLESH
cut 2

PIP
cut 10

OUTER RING
cut 2

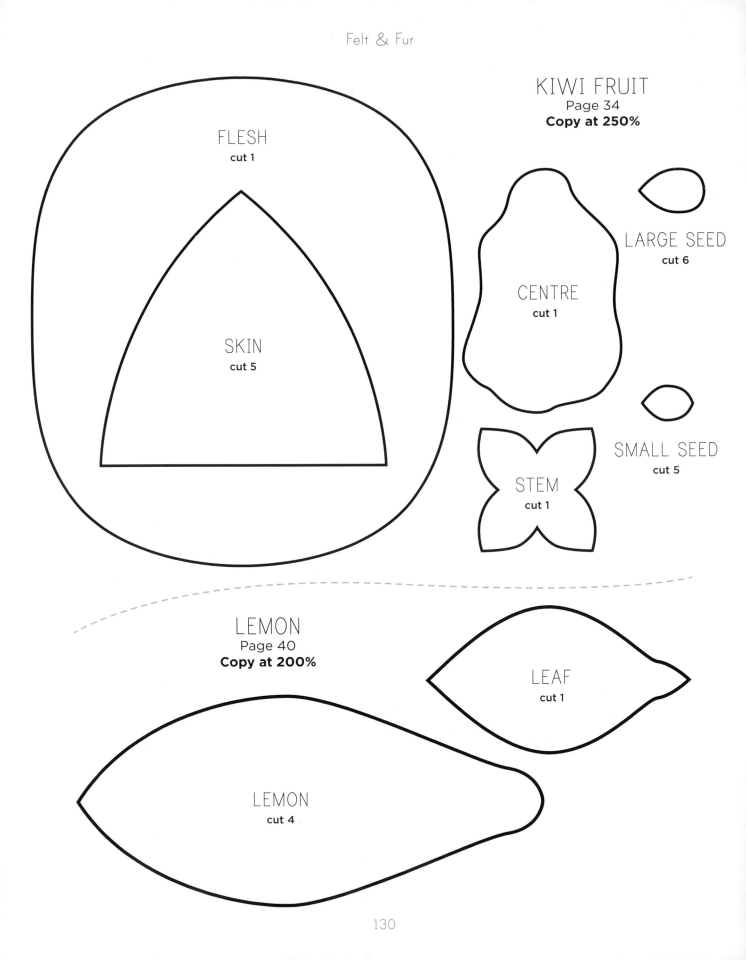

KIWI FRUIT
Page 34
Copy at 250%

FLESH
cut 1

SKIN
cut 5

LARGE SEED
cut 6

CENTRE
cut 1

SMALL SEED
cut 5

STEM
cut 1

LEMON
Page 40
Copy at 200%

LEAF
cut 1

LEMON
cut 4

ACORN
Page 44
Copy at 200%

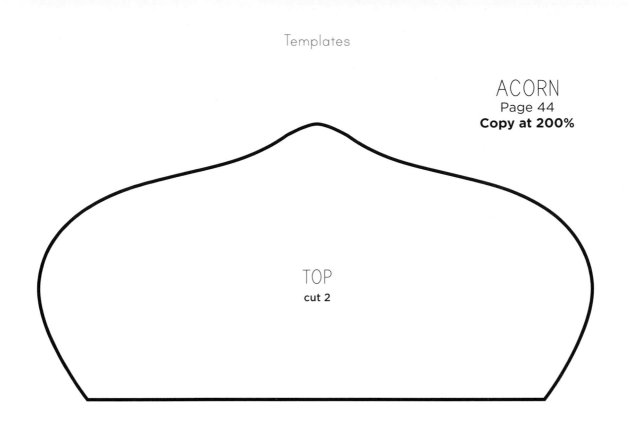

TOP
cut 2

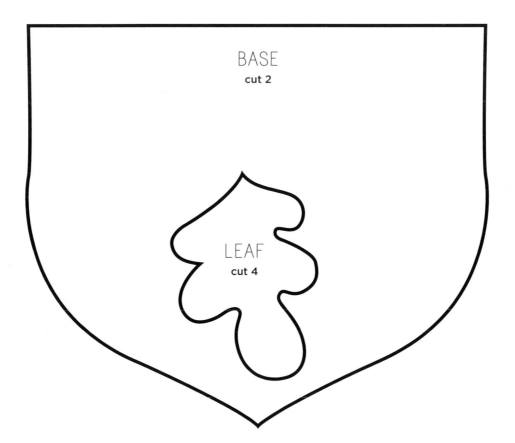

BASE
cut 2

LEAF
cut 4

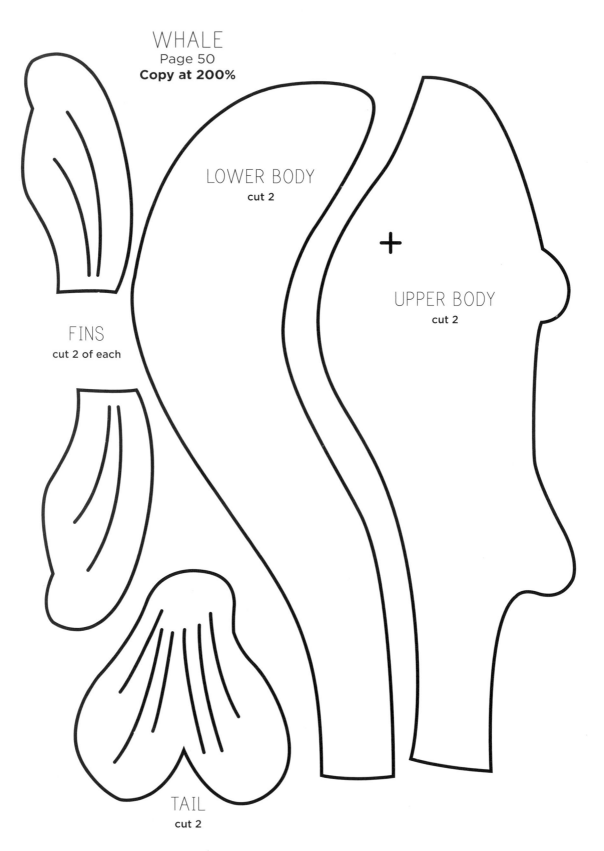

WHALE
Page 50
Copy at 200%

LOWER BODY
cut 2

UPPER BODY
cut 2

FINS
cut 2 of each

TAIL
cut 2

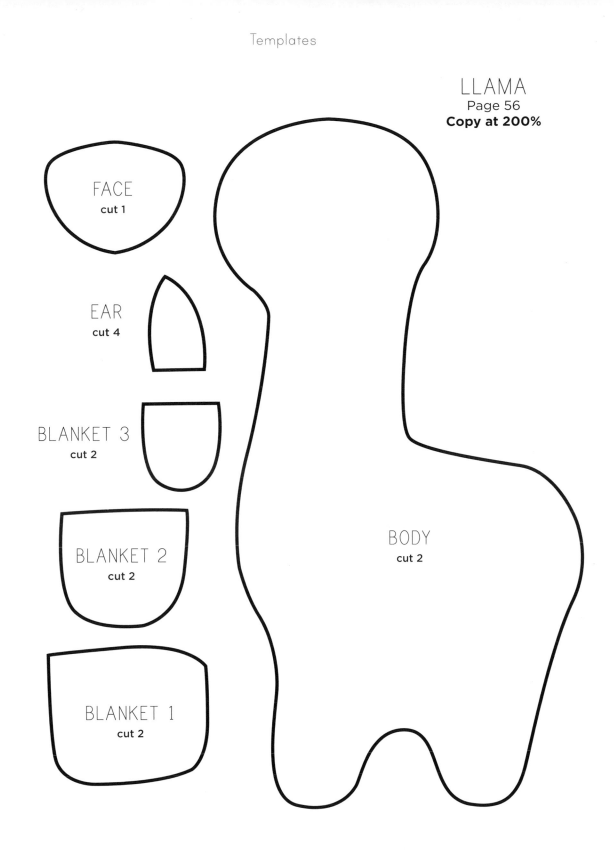

LLAMA
Page 56
Copy at 200%

FACE
cut 1

EAR
cut 4

BLANKET 3
cut 2

BLANKET 2
cut 2

BLANKET 1
cut 2

BODY
cut 2

SUSHI
Page 68
Copy at 200%

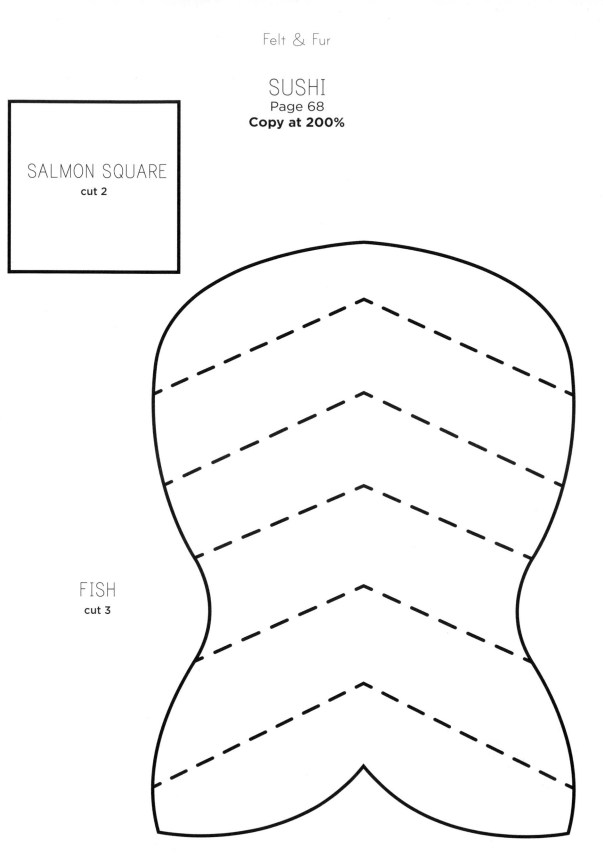

SALMON SQUARE
cut 2

FISH
cut 3

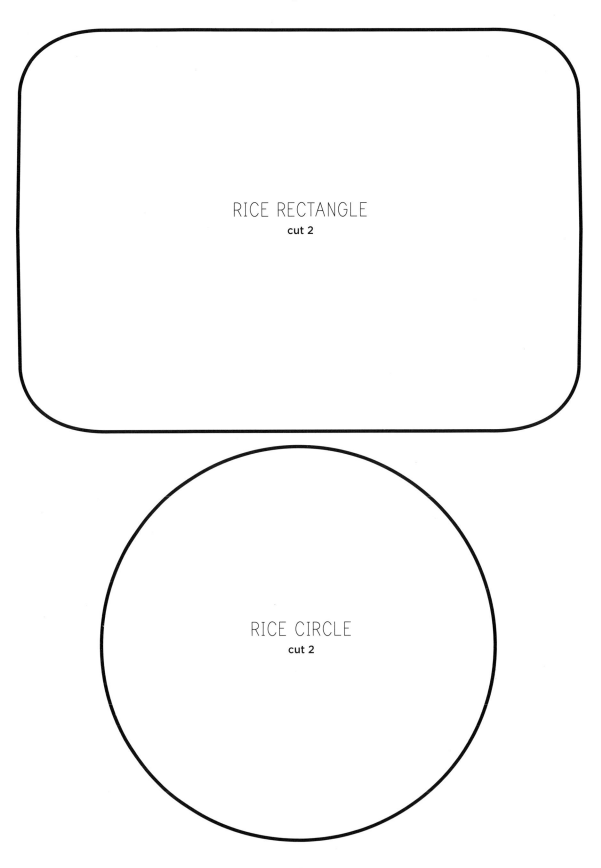

RICE RECTANGLE
cut 2

RICE CIRCLE
cut 2

PEAS IN A POD
Page 74
Copy at 200%

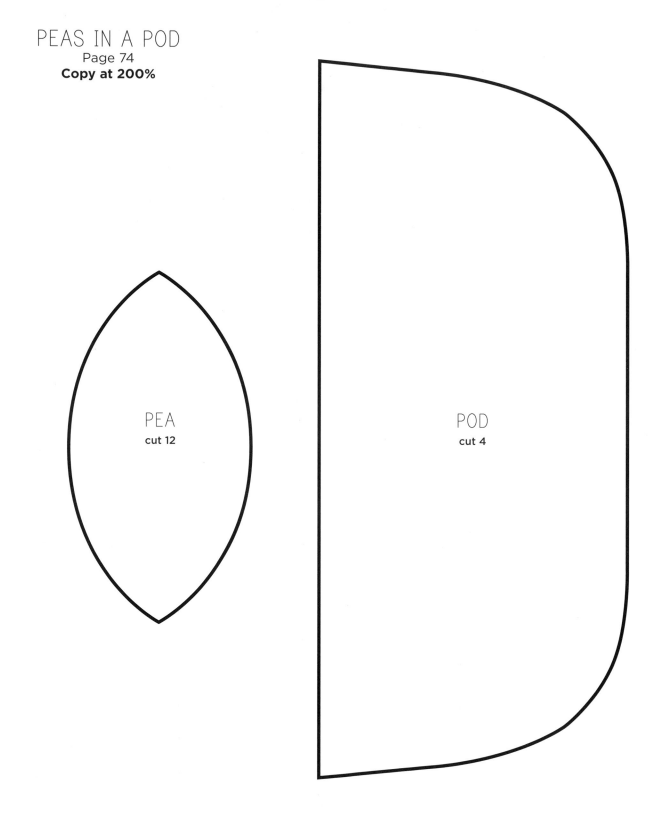

PEA

cut 12

POD

cut 4

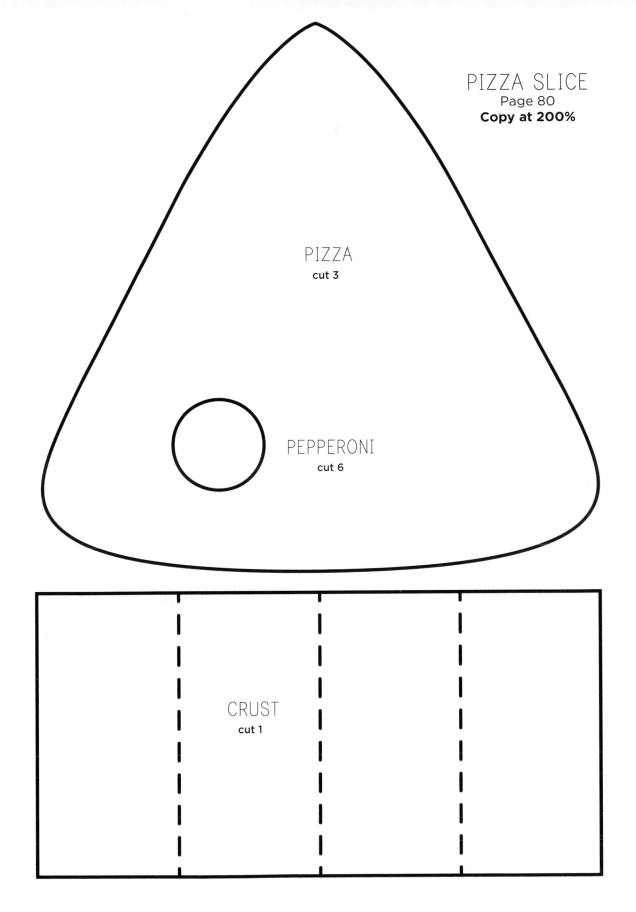

PIZZA SLICE
Page 80
Copy at 200%

PIZZA
cut 3

PEPPERONI
cut 6

CRUST
cut 1

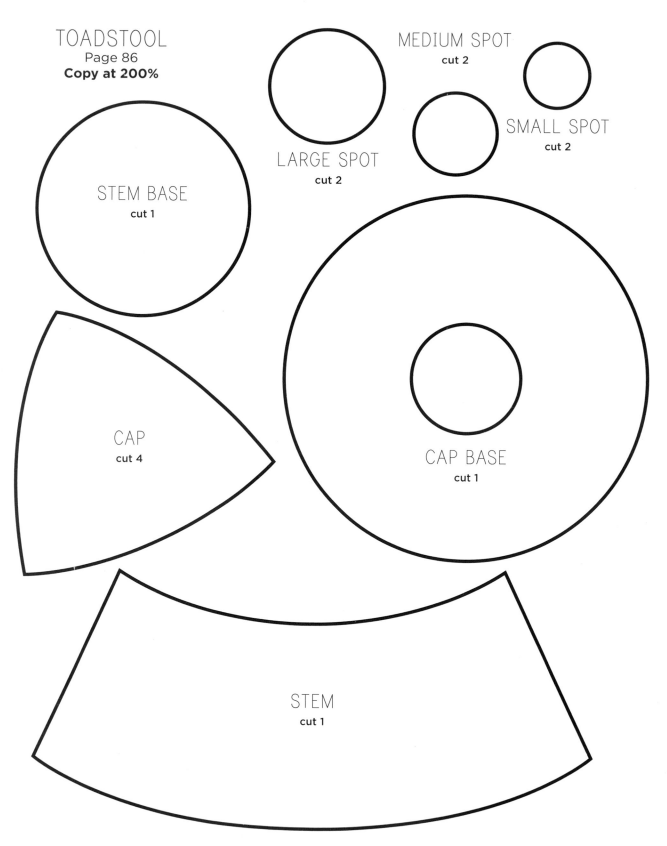

TOADSTOOL
Page 86
Copy at 200%

MEDIUM SPOT
cut 2

SMALL SPOT
cut 2

LARGE SPOT
cut 2

STEM BASE
cut 1

CAP
cut 4

CAP BASE
cut 1

STEM
cut 1

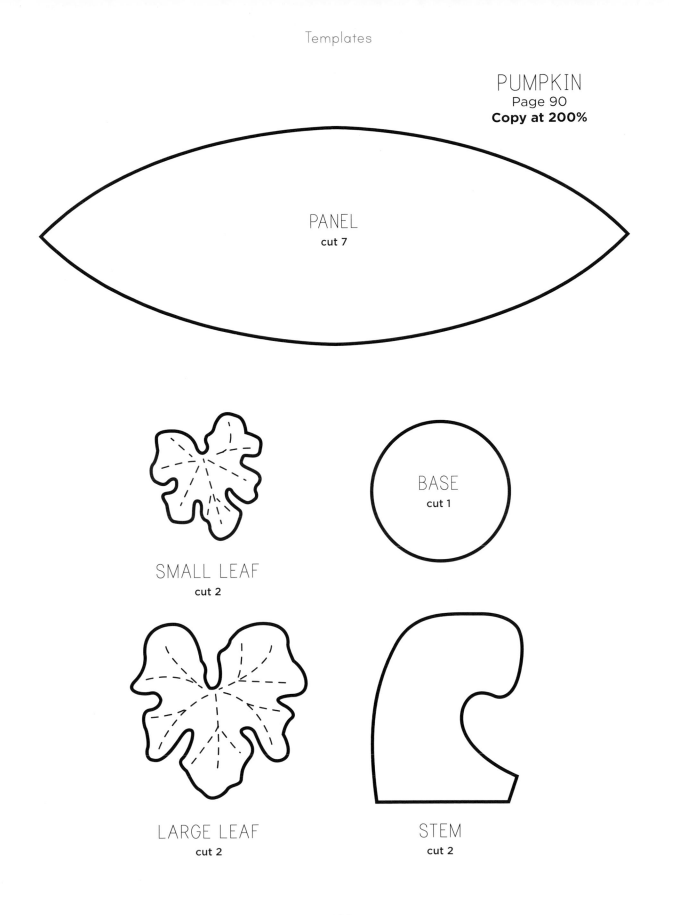

PUMPKIN
Page 90
Copy at 200%

PANEL
cut 7

SMALL LEAF
cut 2

BASE
cut 1

LARGE LEAF
cut 2

STEM
cut 2

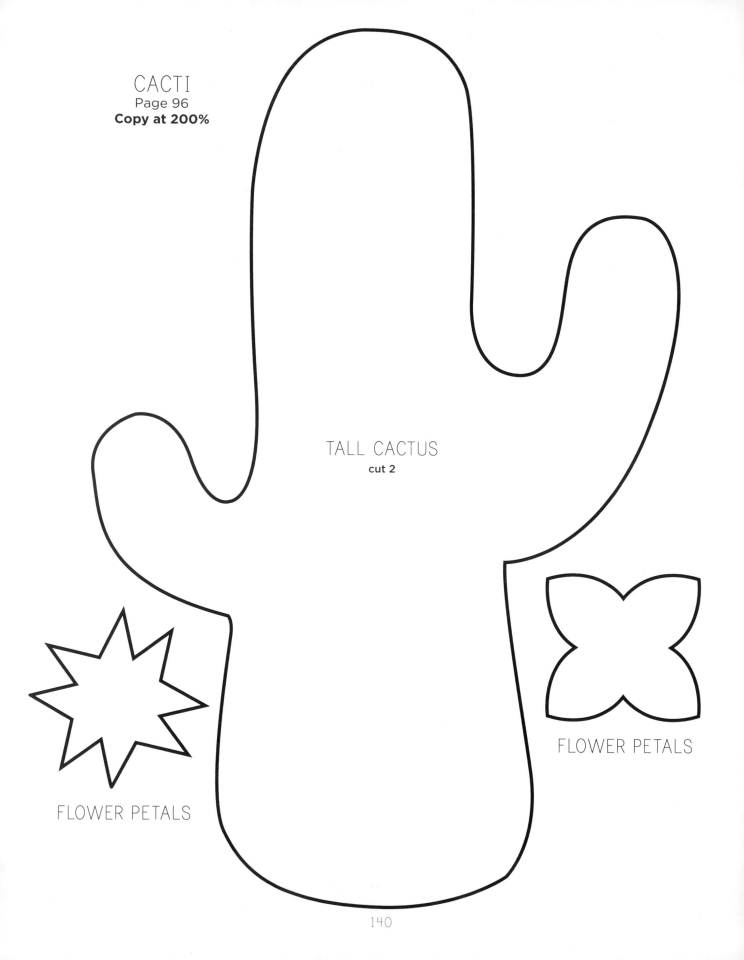

CACTI
Page 96
Copy at 200%

TALL CACTUS

cut 2

FLOWER PETALS

FLOWER PETALS

140

FELT CACTUS
cut 12

FLOWER PETALS

SHORT CACTUS
cut 2

SLOTH
Page 102
Copy at 200%

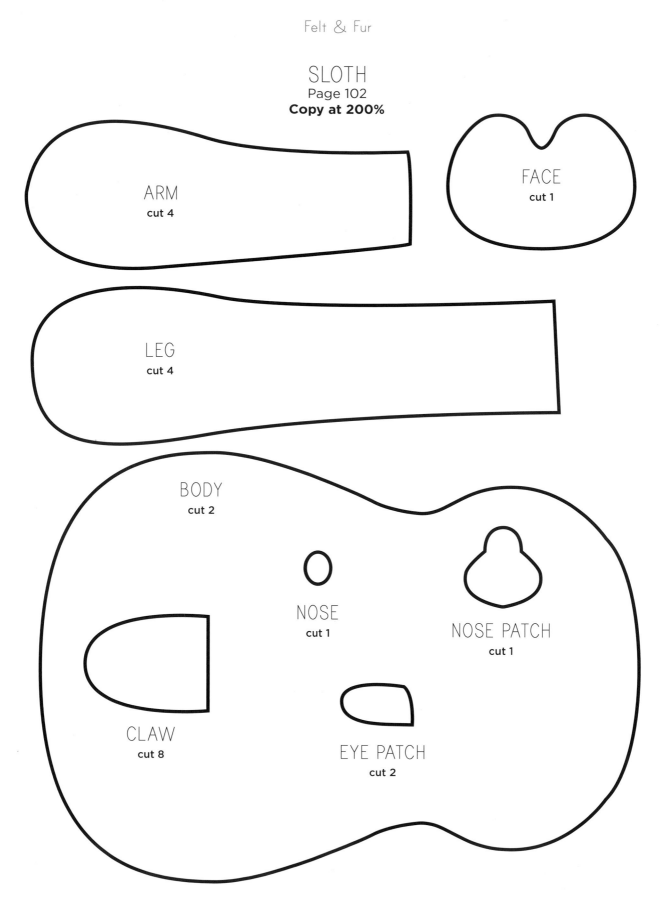

ARM

cut 4

FACE

cut 1

LEG

cut 4

BODY

cut 2

NOSE

cut 1

NOSE PATCH

cut 1

CLAW

cut 8

EYE PATCH

cut 2

SPIDER
Page 108
Copy at 200%

LEGS
cut 4

HEAD
cut 2

HEAD BASE
cut 1

FACE
cut 1

BACK BASE
cut 1

BACK
cut 2

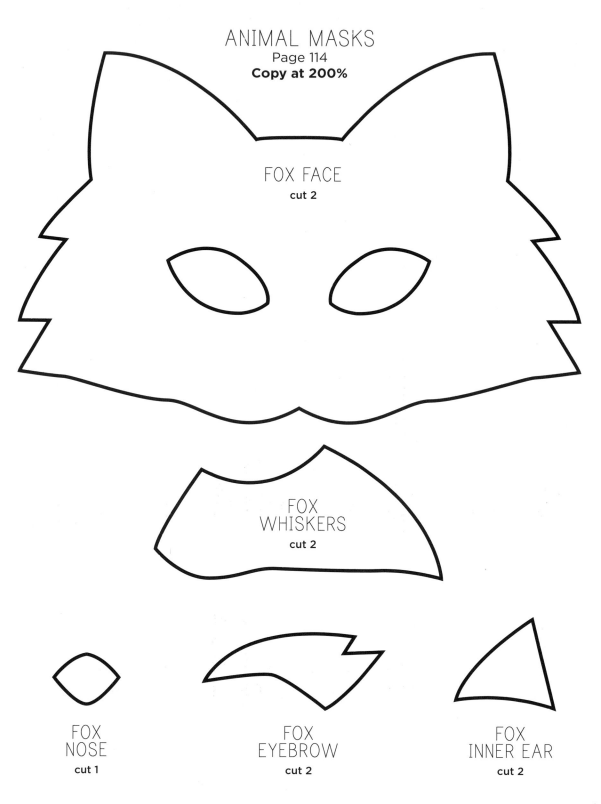

ANIMAL MASKS
Page 114
Copy at 200%

FOX FACE
cut 2

FOX
WHISKERS
cut 2

FOX
NOSE
cut 1

FOX
EYEBROW
cut 2

FOX
INNER EAR
cut 2

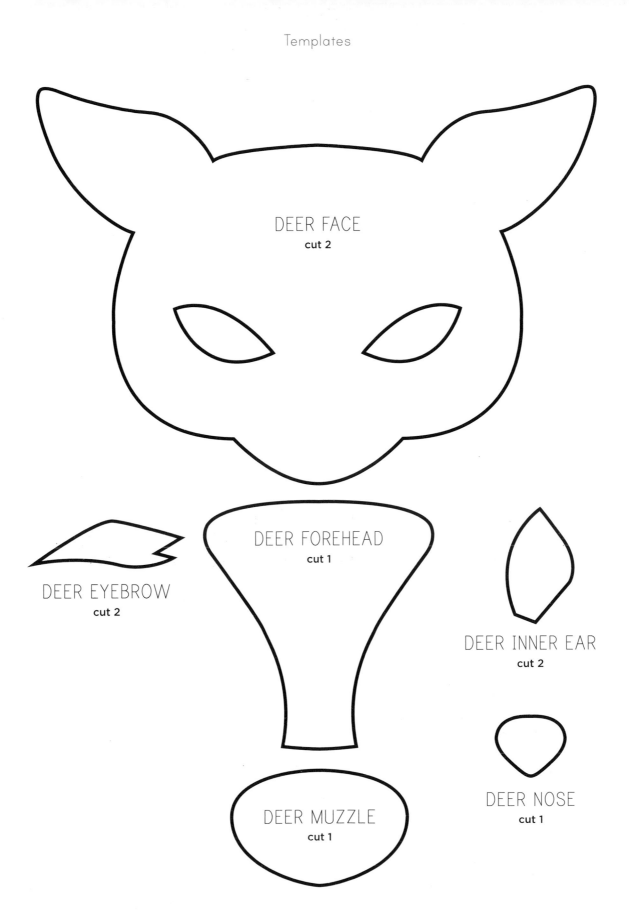

DEER FACE
cut 2

DEER FOREHEAD
cut 1

DEER EYEBROW
cut 2

DEER INNER EAR
cut 2

DEER NOSE
cut 1

DEER MUZZLE
cut 1

ANIMAL MASKS
Page 114
Copy at 200%

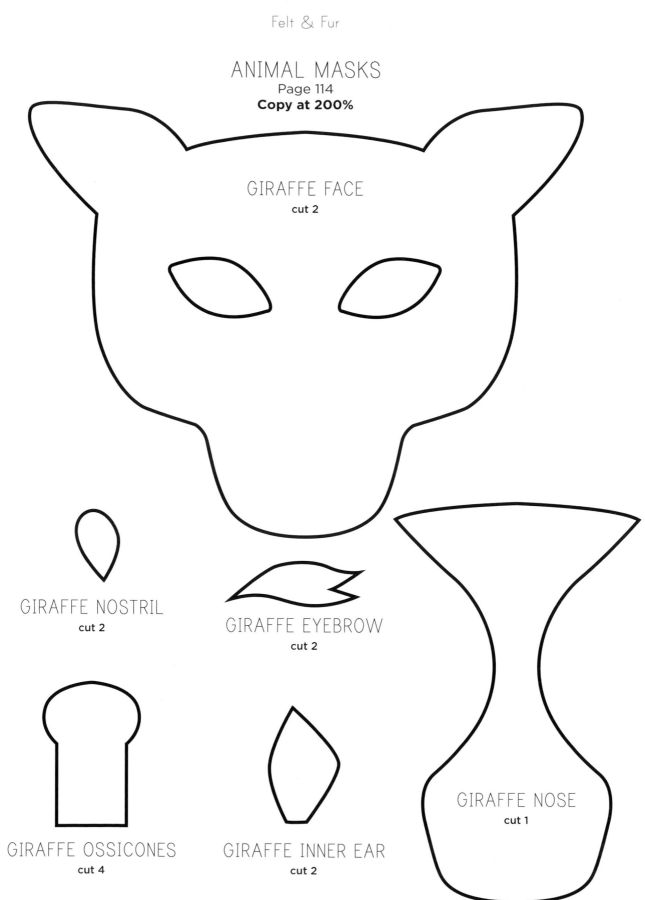

GIRAFFE FACE

cut 2

GIRAFFE NOSTRIL

cut 2

GIRAFFE EYEBROW

cut 2

GIRAFFE OSSICONES

cut 4

GIRAFFE INNER EAR

cut 2

GIRAFFE NOSE

cut 1

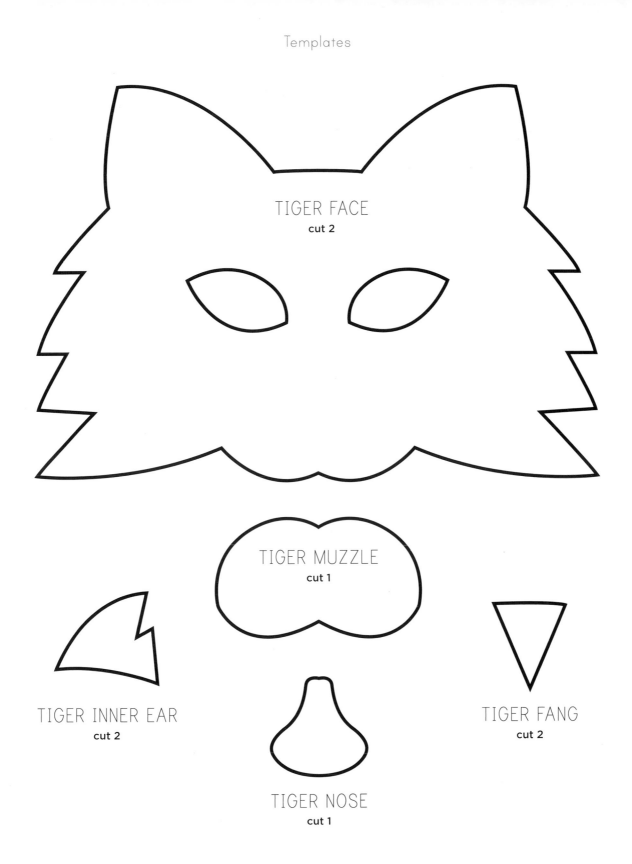

TIGER FACE

cut 2

TIGER MUZZLE

cut 1

TIGER INNER EAR

cut 2

TIGER NOSE

cut 1

TIGER FANG

cut 2

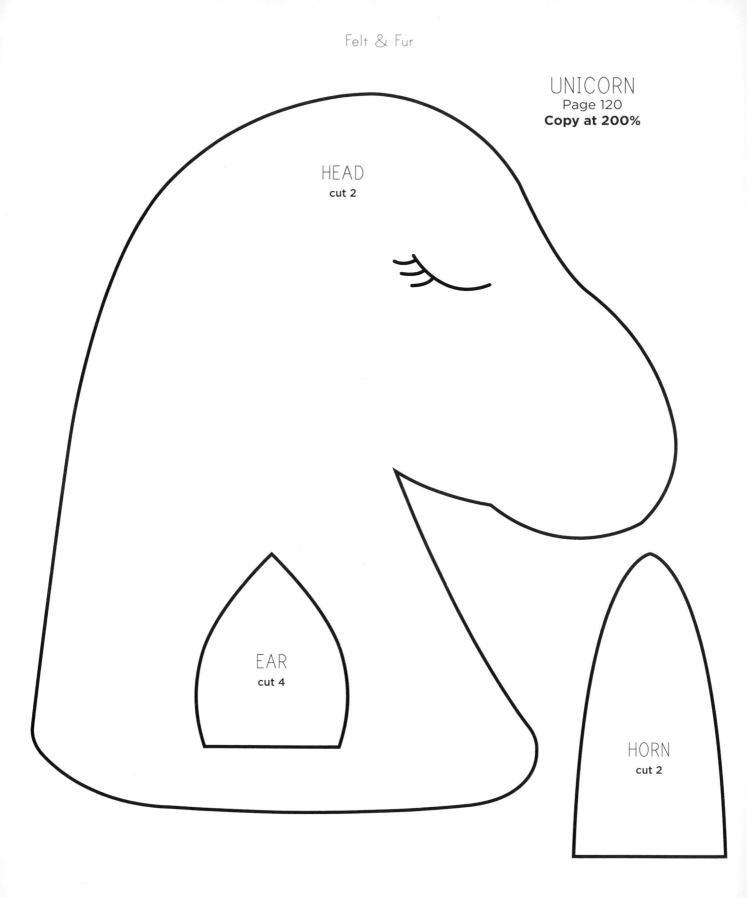

UNICORN
Page 120
Copy at 200%

HEAD
cut 2

EAR
cut 4

HORN
cut 2

RESOURCES

PLUSH, FLEECE, FELT & FUR FABRICS

UK

Plush Addict Ltd
9 Brassey Close
Peterborough
PE1 2AZ
plushaddict.co.uk

UK Fabrics Online
Unit G6, Riverside Suite
Pear Mill
Stockport Road
West Stockport
SK6 2BD
ukfabricsonline.com

myfabrics.co.uk

Hobbycraft
hobbycraft.co.uk

USA

Shannon Fabrics
shannonfabrics.com

fabric.com

The Felt Store
thefeltstore.com

Joann
joann.com

SEWING MACHINES & ACCESSORIES

UK

Sewing Machines Direct
SMD Court Miners Road
Llay Industrial Estate
Wrexham
LL12 0PJ
sewingmachines.co.uk

John Lewis & Partners
johnlewis.com

USA

Joann
joann.com

HABERDASHERY & CRAFT SUPPLIES

UK

Hobbycraft
hobbycraft.co.uk

Fabricland
fabricland.co.uk

Amazon
amazon.co.uk

USA

Michaels
michaels.com

Joann
joann.com

ACKNOWLEDGEMENTS

I would like to thank so many people who have given me guidance, encouragement and support in writing this book.

Firstly, my family, all of you and so many of you – you have been a great part of my life and have nurtured me into the person I am today. To Joe, my lovely, kind husband who is always motivating me to step out of my comfort zone and go for that dream; my children, Will and Lucia, who inspire me every day and are my world; to all my sisters and brothers (yes, there are many); and my amazing nieces and nephews, Rose, Louis, Sof, Eve, Arty and Mabel, who bring so much laughter and crazy ideas into my world. Thank you all.

I would like to say a special thank you to Jonathan Bailey and all the team at GMC Publications for your confidence and faith in working with me once again. Writing my second craft book has been a huge pleasure and your support throughout has been invaluable.

Finally, I am, as always, eternally grateful for the artistic and practical skills I learnt from my mother and father. Without them I never would have had the knowledge and courage to have been able to make a career – let alone write books – based on my creative passions. I'm sure they are looking down on me now, pleased in the knowledge that they had some influence on my future. Thanks Mummsie and Daddsie!

INDEX

First published 2021 by
Guild of Master Craftsman Publications Ltd
Castle Place, 166 High Street, Lewes,
East Sussex BN7 1XU, UK

ISBN 978 1 78494 595 4

Publisher: Jonathan Bailey
Production: Jim Bulley
Editor: Laura Paton
Designer: Robin Shields
Photographer: Andrew Perris
Stylist: Elen Agasiants
Step photography: Emma Herian

Colour origination by GMC Reprographics
Printed and bound in China

To place an order, contact:
GMC Publications
166 High Street, Lewes, East Sussex, BN7 1XU, United Kingdom
+44 (0)1273 488005
www.gmcbooks.com